# NOTES TO NOTES

## How I Went From Music To Real Estate

# NOMI YAH

Notes To Notes:
How I Went From Music To Real Estate

Copyright © 2019 Nomi Yah
All rights reserved
1ˢᵗ Edition, 4ᵗʰ Revision Copyright © 2021

Published by Nomi Yah Music
19050 Bay Street #42, El Verano CA 95433
NomiYahMusic@gmail.com

Written by Nomi Yah

Photographs by Ashton Boni, Mike Lounibos, Peter Salmon

Cover Design & Book Design by Nomi Yah

| | |
|---|---|
| Publisher: | Nomi Yah Music |
| Title: | Notes To Notes |
| Subtitle: | How I Went From Music To Real Estate |
| Distribution: | KDP Publishing |
| ISBN: | 9781091717244 |

# Notes To Notes

## How I Went From Music To Real Estate

Nomi Yah

# Dedication

This book is dedicated:

To my grandfather Henry Milner, my mother Nicole Milner and my stepfather Karl Linn, for the inspiration and impact their lives had on mine;

To my son Malaika Wanag, for suggesting I write this book, for putting up with me while I was living it, and for being the best part of my life;

To my father Harold Ginsberg, for believing in me and giving me a start in the note business. When I told him I was writing a book, he responded by quoting the Bible, "Of making many books there is no end and much study wearies the body."

# CONTENTS

**Chapter 1**                                **Page**    1
GRANDPA WAS AN ENTREPRENEUR

**Chapter 2**                                **Page**    23
CHILD OF THE FLOWER CHILDREN

**Chapter 3**                                **Page**    43
ON THE BACKS OF ANGELS

**Chapter 4**                                **Page**    55
THE MUSIC BUSINESS

**Chapter 5**                                **Page**    89
MY FAMILY

**Chapter 6**                                **Page**    113
ON TOUR

**Chapter 7**                                **Page**    141
DOCUMENT ORGANIZER

**Chapter 8**                      **Page 159**
REAL ESTATE

**Chapter 9**                      **Page 179**
ELOHE LOANS

**Chapter 10**                   **Page 189**
ON NOTES TO NOTES

**Appendix 1**                  **Page 201**
EXAMPLES

**Appendix 2**                  **Page 213**
BIBLIOGRAPHY

**Appendix 3**                  **Page 223**
NOMI YAH BIOGRAPHY

**Appendix 4**                  **Page 235**
NICOLE MILNER BIOGRAPHY

**Appendix 5**                  **Page 239**
KARL LINN BIOGRAPHY

**Appendix 6**                  **Page 249**
LYRICS

MY STUDIO

MY GOLD RECORD

A GIG IN SAN JOSE

A GIG IN SEATTLE

# Chapter 1

# GRANDPA WAS AN ENTREPRENEUR

Grandpa was a major influence on my life. He was a successful self-made entrepreneur and he started multiple businesses and factories. His stories imprinted on me how to create and run a business. He inspired me to believe that I could work for myself and not be an employee.

His example showed me how to create something from nothing, even while going through immense challenges. He taught me how to achieve goals in spite of all obstacles.

Grandpa's drive to succeed was what I thought of as The Bulldozer Effect. His example taught me to be a bulldozer too and this led to success in the music industry and in real estate.

Grandpa developed The Bulldozer Effect by overcoming a series of difficulties as a young man. His name was Henry Milner and he was born in Poland. After high school, he enrolled in university. The first day of class, he was called into the dean's office for what he thought was his official welcome into university.

When he went into the office, the dean was sitting behind a desk and two large men were standing. The dean got up from the chair and walked over to him. Grandpa smiled and held out his hand in greeting. The dean didn't smile and he didn't shake hands. He sternly told Grandpa he wasn't welcome at the school. It was for Polish citizens and not for Jews.

Grandpa was stunned and didn't know how to respond. The dean abruptly left the room. The two large men blocked Grandpa's way and shut the door. They started punching and beating him up. They warned him not to come back, then let him go.

He ran home and told his parents. They discussed the situation and all agreed, he would have to leave Poland. His plan was to go to business school, start a business, then bring his family to come live with him. He said goodbye and moved to Paris and later to Brussels.

He found a job opening for a position at a suitcase factory. He told them he had experience working in a suitcase factory in Poland. He said the quality of work in Poland didn't match the high standards in Belgium so, even though he was experienced, he would still have to be trained on their superior equipment. The story worked and they hired him.

He got a scholarship for business school. He went to school and worked part-time in the suitcase factory. On weekends, he went door-to-door selling radios. He ate full meals only a couple of times a week. Most days he only had bread to eat. He couldn't afford butter, so he warmed up chicken fat to put on the bread. He sprinkled it with plenty of salt and pepper to make it taste a little better.

He heard that rubber was a good business and found a job at a rubber factory. He befriended the foreman and they socialized outside work. One evening after work, Grandpa suggested they start their own company. They talked until late at night and the

3

foreman told him about an invention he had designed.

That weekend, Grandpa went to the foreman's house to see the invention. It was a machine that made rubber shoes in multiple colors. At the time, rubber shoes were popular, but factories could only make them one solid color. This invention was something completely new and innovative.

He asked if the invention was patented and the foreman said it wasn't. He said he didn't want to deal with it and wasn't interested in running a business. He offered to give the machine and the rights to Grandpa, who was amazed that he was being given such an opportunity. The foreman drew up papers giving him the rights.

Grandpa applied for a patent and began researching how to build a factory. He consulted with the foreman and other colleagues at the rubber factory. They advised him about what kind of building and equipment he would need to construct his own factory. They told him where he could get rubber and other supplies.

His colleagues made him a couple of samples, secretly using the rubber factory's equipment and materials. He took the samples to wholesalers and offered to sell the product at 75% off retail. There was a lot of interest, even though they would have to wait for their orders to be manufactured. He had them sign for their orders in writing, with advance deposits. He got a half dozen orders and deposits before he had even started production.

He took the orders and went to the biggest bank in Brussels. He asked the teller if he could speak to the president. She wanted to know the purpose and he said he was there to get a loan for four million francs. She asked him to wait a moment and left. Then she came back and escorted him into the president's office.

The bank president was sitting behind a big shiny desk and he asked Grandpa why the loan request was so large. Grandpa laid his documents on the desk. He pointed to the orders and the patent papers, explaining his plan to build a rubber shoe factory. The bank president was impressed and agreed to lend him four million francs. He said his son needed a career and asked if he could be a partner.

Grandpa was taken aback. He didn't actually want to borrow that much from a bank. It would have been too much debt for a start-up company. He had asked for a high number, figuring they would settle on a smaller amount. He asked the banker to give him the offer in writing and said he'd come back the following day and let him know.

He took the offer from the bank and the rest of his documents and went to visit one of his friends. His friend had recently married into a wealthy family and got excited when he heard about the business opportunity. Now that he was married to an ultra-wealthy heiress, he had nothing to do. He'd been searching for an opportunity like this. He liked the idea of being a manufacturer and businessman. He offered to invest the entire four million francs.

Grandpa had a counter proposal. His education in business served him well and he seized the moment to create the best company he could. He proposed they have three equal partners. The friend would own one-third and invest 1,500,000 francs. The banker's son would own one-third and also invest 1,500,000 francs.

Of course, Grandpa had no money to invest, but owning the patent was valued to be worth 500,000 francs. The remaining 1,000,000 francs would come from the bank loan. Grandpa would have the right to purchase stock up to one-third and, when he paid off the bank loan, he would have full partnership.

The three partners agreed to the terms. The partnership agreement included a sizable salary to compensate Grandpa for being the General Manager. He continued to live modestly and put aside most of his salary to purchase stock. Soon he was a full equal partner.

The newly formed company bought five acres near the airport. It had an existing factory that they retrofitted. Grandpa hired most of his colleagues at the other rubber factory and doubled their salary. His inventor friend became the Technical Supervisor, with a salary many times higher than what he was making as foreman at the other factory, plus a royalty on every sale. The company employed around eighty people. Some of the employees lived in little houses on the property.

They built an important business that was visited by the King of Belgium. It had taken three months to get into production and, only three years later, it became publicly traded. Grandpa had made it, all his work finally paid off. He bought a house and a car. He took his wife and daughter on vacations to the south of France. He brought his relatives from Poland to live with him, fulfilling the promise he'd made to them years before. He was a self-made success.

As a well-respected factory owner, he was exactly the kind of wealthy Jewish businessman that was a target during World War Two. He'd come to Western Europe to escape racism in Eastern Europe, but he faced racism again in a much more dangerous form. Belgium had declared itself neutral in the war and they were unprepared, early one morning in 1940, when they were ambushed and the German military began attacking the border.

Late that night, a friend in the Belgium government knocked on Grandpa's door. Grandpa's ambition and hard work had elevated him into a wealthy social circle. He had many friends who were successful and influential. The friend who came that night had seen Grandpa's name on the enemy's "most wanted list". He said it was urgent to leave immediately and warned Grandpa not to wait until the bank was open in the morning, to get out right away with whatever money he had in the house.

Grandpa had some gold coins and cash hidden in the house. He split the money equally and they sewed it into bags. They tied the bags on each family member under their clothing. There were seven of them, five adults and two children. They piled into the car and left their home in the middle of the night. My mom was three-years-old.

They went to the train station and there were already thousands of people trying to get out. France had closed the border. Grandpa drove the family to a hospital and bribed an ambulance driver to hide the family in back. The driver put on the siren and crossed the border. Several hours later, Brussels was bombed.

When they got to Dunkirk, it was even worse than Belgium. There were enemy planes flying overhead and Grandpa swore the planes flew so close, he could see the blue eyes of the pilots. It took Mom years to understand why her heart raced whenever a plane flew overhead, even though she wasn't afraid of flying.

Grandpa approached people and offered to buy their car. He'd pay double what it was worth, as long as it had a full tank of gas. He finally found someone willing to sell him a car. He drove until the car ran out of gas and then bought another one that had a full tank. In this way, he managed to drive across France, avoiding cities and large roads. They went south toward the border of Spain.

When they got to Bayonne, Grandpa found an apartment to rent. Bayonne was a small beach town and he thought it would be a safe place to wait out the war. But soon he learned that small villages were being bombed too and he realized they would have to leave Europe.

My grandmother didn't want to go. She refused to leave her country, she was French, and insisted on staying. Grandpa wasn't able to convince her to come with them. She stayed in France and changed her name to pass as a Gentile. Thankfully, she survived the war, but she never saw her daughter again.

Many decades later, with the help of a private detective, we were reunited with the lost French branch of the family. We met Mom's first cousins, who looked like her. They didn't know they were half-Jewish. I saw my first photographs of my grandmother and she looked exactly like me.

Grandpa was sad to say goodbye to my grandmother, but the most urgent thing in his mind was to escape the war as quickly as possible. He went to the international consulates in Bordeaux. He went into one after another and didn't care which country it was. He was finally able to bribe someone at the El Salvadorian consulate for passports and visas. On Grandpa's passport, he changed his name from Henry Milner to Henrique Milnero.

The family traveled to Lisbon and arrived in the afternoon. It was early enough to make it to the American consulate before it closed. Grandpa left the family at a hotel and found his way to the American consulate. He told the receptionist he was going to visit his family in El Salvador. He asked for a twenty-four hour transit visa to change to another ship in New York City.

The receptionist left and went into a private office. A few minutes later she returned, followed by the consulate. He had a wide smile on his face. He asked, "Is your father Juan Milnero from El Salvador?" Grandpa went along with it and said, "Yes that's my father." The consulate shook his hand and said he was a good friend of his parents. He'd been to their house in El Salvador.

The consulate stamped the passports with visas for six months in America. Grandpa thanked him and then asked for another favor. There was a long waiting list for ships and he needed help getting tickets to El Salvador. The consulate made a phone call and got him tickets on a ship, leaving in two days. They walked out of the building together and shook hands warmly.

When Grandpa left through the gates, a number of Jewish refugees approached him. They'd seen him with the consulate and it looked like they were personal friends. They asked Grandpa to help them escape from the war and he was sad that there was nothing he could do for them. He couldn't tell them he wasn't who he appeared to be.

He hurried back to the hotel, feeling relief that now he finally had passports, visas and tickets. He didn't notice when his moneybag slipped out and fell on the sidewalk. A man saw it fall and ran to catch up and give it back to him. It was memorable that someone was honest and civil in a time of war.

Two days later, my family was on a ship sailing across the Atlantic Ocean. They stayed in the cabin most of the time and kept to themselves. They needed to avoid interacting with anyone who might find out they had fake passports.

When they got to New York, everyone was told to get off on Ellis Island and go through U.S. immigration. Grandpa was afraid to get off and have his fake passports discovered. United States was sending Jews back to Europe, they weren't accepting refugees in 1940.

Grandpa refused to get off at Ellis Island. He yelled, in an imitation Salvadorian accent, that he wasn't going to America and didn't have time to go through U.S. Customs. He waved his tickets and passports, shouting about missing his connection to El Salvador.

Everyone had gotten off the ship, except the employees and my family. Grandpa wouldn't get off and threatened to sue. He kept yelling and screaming until they finally let the family stay onboard. After docking in the harbor in New York City, several of the crew members carried the luggage out to the street and hailed a taxi, so my family could hurry and catch the next ship. But instead, they stayed in America.

Grandpa and Mom were lucky to get to the United States. But it wasn't just luck. It was the grace of God, and the kindness of heroes, who helped save my family. Most of all, it was Grandpa's creative problem solving, his grit and determination. The Bulldozer Effect.

We lost many members of our family in that terrible war. All who lived through that time were scarred for life. My cousin was imprisoned in a concentration camp. She had a tattoo of a number on her forearm, literally scarred for life. She escaped the camp through an opening in the fence. She walked all night and hid all day, stealing food and eating leaves. She kept track of the sun's position and kept heading toward the south. She walked from Germany to Italy and was able to get on a boat to Haifa. When I met her, she still lived in Israel.

My stepfather Karl Linn was born near Berlin into a family of farmers. They were forced to leave the country and were accepted to Palestine as refugees. He grew up there and later became an American citizen. He had an illustrious career as a landscape architect. He designed the interior landscaping for the Four Seasons in New York City. He is considered the founder of the urban gardening movement. He and Mom were interviewed in the film *Multiply By Six Million* about their personal stories.

Grandpa succeeded in escaping the war, but his struggle was not over. He had no money left, he'd spent the equivalent of one-hundred-thousand dollars in two months. He'd been wealthy, with a home and possessions, a factory and a bank account. But all of it was stolen from him. He didn't even have his wife anymore and was suddenly a single father.

He was in a desperate fight to rebuild and survive. It was stressful, but he didn't complain. He considered himself lucky and was grateful to be in the United States. Years later, he was proud when he and his daughter became citizens. He felt honored to vote and serve on juries. After he retired, he put on a suit once a week and volunteered at the Small Business Association, giving advice to entrepreneurs.

He had to figure out how to make a living immediately. He worked as a street food vendor and enrolled in a night class to learn English. It wasn't difficult for him to learn a new language, he already spoke French, Polish, Russian, Yiddish and Flemish. He worked hard to minimize his accent, knowing it would make a big difference in business.

He was downtown and he saw a radio in a store window. It had a big round speaker in front. He wondered what happened to the round piece of wood they cut out to make room for the speaker. He wrote down the name of the radio company and called the operator to get the address.

He visited the radio factory and asked to speak to the foreman. He inquired what they did with the round pieces of wood they cut out. The foreman answered they paid someone to cart the pieces away. Grandpa offered to cart them away at half the price and the foreman agreed.

Grandpa got paid to pick up the wood circles, but he didn't throw them away. He used the money he was paid to hire a few people. They sanded the wood and painted the edges in bright colors. He took samples and went to sell them, saying they were handcrafted cutting boards. He managed to get them into several stores, including Woolworth's, the largest department store at the time. But the cutting boards started cracking and customers returned them. The business shut down and Grandpa had to figure out something else.

He was in a hardware store and noticed some little boxes of screws and nails. Each box was full of a single size of fastener. From his experience in factories, he knew there must be some irregulars and he wondered what happened to the ones that were not exactly identical. He wrote down the name of the factory that was printed on the boxes. He found the address and went to visit.

He asked to speak to the foreman and wanted to know what happened to the irregulars. The foreman answered that they couldn't sell irregulars and had to pay someone to haul them away. Grandpa offered to haul them away at half the price. The foreman agreed to give the contract to Grandpa.

They paid him to pick up the irregulars, but he didn't haul them to the dump. He bought a case of little boxes and his employees filled the boxes with a mixture of screws and nails. They glued on labels that said "Assortment Fasteners". He claims that he was the first person to invent the Assortment category for hardware. But the business was slow and there wasn't enough demand.

Eventually, he got into the women's raincoat business and built another factory. He repeated the steps he'd taken in Brussels. First he got a job in a raincoat factory. Then he worked and hustled his way up, until he had his own factory and his own designs. His raincoats were popular in Sears, Woolworth's and other stores.

After everything he went through, he was able to get back on his feet. He never became as wealthy as he was before the war, but he did well enough to be comfortable. He remarried and they lived in a nice apartment with a doorman, on Lexington Avenue and East 88$^{th}$ Street. When they got older, they could afford to retire in Florida.

Growing up, I visited Manhattan nearly every summer. Grandpa always bought tickets for me to watch Broadway plays. I saw classics like *Pippen* and *The King And I*. Later I wrote several musicals.

Grandpa put on a suit whenever he went to the bank. He'd take me along, pointing out how elegant the building was and how the bank president knew him personally. He was proud of his businesses and told me stories. He emphasized that the most important person to have on a business team was an accountant. His accountant was his personal best friend for many years.

He didn't hide that he had tricked people. He wasn't ashamed of doing what he had to do to survive. He wasn't always honest, but he was careful to never hurt anyone. He smiled and laughed when he talked about how he got away with something, like he was bragging, proud of his cleverness.

Grandpa inspired me to become an entrepreneur when I was only eight-years-old, and I continued working as I was growing up. There seemed to be an endless number of services people would pay for. Stacking firewood. Feeding chickens. Babysitting. Giving piano lessons. Creating puppet shows and selling tickets. Training ponies for children to ride. Rolling joints for grown ups, two for a dollar, even though I didn't smoke. Selling calligraphy on the sidewalk, pretending to write a customer's name in Chinese and charging a dollar for the counterfeits.

A few times, I experienced being an employee when I was a teenager. I scooped ice cream in a shop on Main Street and cleaned rooms in a bed and breakfast. But the jobs didn't pay as well as working for myself. Being an entrepreneur was more profitable than having a job and allowed for more freedom. That was a lesson I learned early in life.

I was around twelve-years-old and I was visiting Manhattan. Grandpa asked me to come into his office, close the door and sit down. His face was very serious and he talked for a long time. He told me he'd made more money than he needed. He'd worked many extra years so that he could leave an inheritance to his grandchildren. It wasn't as much as he would have liked, he reminded me about losing everything in the war.

He asked me what I would do if I inherited some money. Then he abruptly stopped talking and waited for me to answer. He looked at me intensely and it was intimidating. I wracked my brain for something to say that would sound responsible and mature.

The only thing I could think of, that would cost a large sum of money and be practical, was a house. I said I'd use my inheritance for a down payment on a house. I could either live in it or rent it out.

Grandpa's face lit up in a big smile. He said he agreed that real estate was a wise investment. He was a sharply critical man and that moment may have been the only time he ever gave me approval. He always made his opinions known. He didn't approve of the music business. He did approve of real estate investing.

# Chapter 2

# Child Of The Flower Children

My mom was a musician and her name was Nicole Milner. She was a composer and songwriter, known for playing with great sensitivity. Mom was kind, compassionate, intelligent, etc. Even a long list of remarkable adjectives wouldn't begin to describe her. Mom was my music teacher and my best friend.

She would help people she didn't even know. Several times she lent money to people who were a little short on a down payment to buy a house. Once she heard about an acquaintance that needed emergency surgery to save her eyesight, but couldn't afford it and there wasn't enough time to put together a fundraiser. Mom paid for the surgery with her credit card and the woman's eyesight was saved.

Mom was strikingly beautiful. One time, I was at the Kodak Theater in Hollywood for an awards show. The lobby was lined with giant portraits of movie stars and I froze when I saw the photograph of Audrey Hepburn. I thought it was a picture of Mom.

She was an exceptional pianist. As a child she studied classical music and attended The High School Of Music And Art, where she made a record for her senior project. After she turned eighteen, she could get into jazz clubs and was introduced to improvisation. Improvising became her trademark and every performance was unique. She described it as being "tuned in to the energy".

Over the years, she shared many of her deep insights about music. Music is creation, not memorization. An artist who is fully present transmits that to the audience and triggers them to "be here now". A performance is a communion of people experiencing the moment together, like a group meditation or a religious gathering.

When Mom was nine-years-old, her father bought her a used baby grand piano. They were living on Riverside Drive in New York. Around seventy years later, I inherited that piano and moved it to Riverside Drive in California.

Some of my earliest memories were of that baby grand. I crawled around under it and listened to Mom play. I wasn't tall enough to see the piano keys, but I could reach up and press a key with my fingertip and hear the sound. The bench was too high to climb and Mom picked me up to sit beside her. She showed me which keys to press to play *Mary Had A Little Lamb*. Mom taught me to read music and the alphabet at the same time, before I was in kindergarten. If music was a language, I was bilingual.

My family moved a lot, mostly following my dad's career. I was born in the Bronx, New York. We lived down the block from the hospital where I was born, where Dad attended Albert Einstein Medical School. My older brother was two-years-old when I was born.

When I was six-months-old, we moved to Florida and I had my first memory, a huge face was looking into my crib in a sunny room. At one-year-old, we moved to Los Angeles, where we had a circular driveway and towering cypress trees. We had tortoises in the backyard that my parents told me not to ride. My little brother was born.

Dad was drafted during the Vietnam War. I was five-years-old when he went to basic training in San Antonio, Texas. I remember climbing a ladder up a zip-line tower. Soldiers in uniform strapped me into a harness and pushed me off the tower. I went down fast and it was scary for a few seconds. But then Dad was there, reaching his arms out, and he caught me.

Dad was stationed in North Carolina for two years. As we drove into the state, Mom read a sign out loud that said, "Welcome to North Carolina, Klan Country". She looked upset and spoke urgently to Dad. I was too young to understand what they were saying.

I attended kindergarten and first grade in Fayetteville. Every day, the teacher got angry with the same three children. The children didn't misbehave and I didn't know why the teacher got so mad. When she got angry, her face became scary. She spoke sternly and sent those three children to the office to get paddled. A little while later, they came back to the class crying. This happened to them every day.

Many years passed before I recognized that what I had witnessed was racism. They were the only black children in the class. The white children never got paddled. It was all the more sinister because it was a teacher. All I understood at the time was that, whenever she talked to me, she was a nice lady. But when she talked to those three children, she turned into a scary monster. That's when I started having nightmares.

When I was seven-years-old, we drove across country in a wood-paneled station wagon. We brought our Siamese cat and she escaped the car at a gas station, it took over an hour to find her. We stopped at the Grand Canyon and the overwhelming vastness made me dizzy.

When we got to Los Angeles, we didn't stay there very long. My parents decided to raise their children in the country instead of the city. We started driving north, on a quest to find a place to relocate. We drove to Big Sur and camped under the redwoods by the ocean.

My parents discussed moving there because it was beautiful. But it was cold and rainy the whole time, so we kept going.

We got to San Francisco and went to PlayLand At The Beach, an old-fashioned amusement park that closed a few years later. We drove over the Golden Gate Bridge and Dad pointed to Alcatraz and told us about the prison. We drove for several hours on windy roads.

We finally came to the remote coastal village of Mendocino. The whole town seemed to be floating on a cloud and glowing in the sun. Dad pulled the car off Highway One, onto a lookout point. We could see the entire town from there, because it jutted out on a little peninsula. A layer of fog sat low over the ocean, but the town itself was clear and sunny. The effect made it seem like a magical village floating on a cloud. Mom declared this would be where we were going to live.

Mendocino was a dramatically beautiful, historical village with church steeples, Old West storefronts and boardwalks instead of sidewalks. An old-fashioned hotel had horse hitches in front and a wooden hand-painted sign hanging from rusty chains. The sign said

"Victuals", but Dad said it was pronounced "Vittles".

We lived in rentals outside town. Soon we moved to the center of town into a semi-Victorian house. It was a two-story enchanted-looking home. There were secret passageways to other bedrooms through the closets. Upstairs was a laundry chute that went downstairs and we weren't supposed to jump down, but we did.

From our house, I could walk everywhere, to school, the store, the beach. Dad opened a psychiatry office in town. I loved living in the little village of Mendocino. I always imagined how differently my life might have turned out if I'd grown up there.

My family bought forty acres of meadow and redwoods and built a house. It was twenty minutes south of Mendocino, in the neighboring hamlet of Albion. We moved from the middle of town to the middle of nowhere, at the end of Middle Ridge Road.

My parents hired a man who was known as a water witch. He used a Y-shaped stick to find a location to dig a well. He walked around our land until the stick moved, he said to dig a well there. That well produced water ever since. During the drought, neighbors came to fill containers. Their wells had dried out and ours never did.

When the house was finished, the living room had an open beam ceiling, swooping up to a wall of big windows. I played piano with a view looking out over a forested canyon. A porch wrapped all the way around the house and there was a tire swing in the yard. My bedroom was on the corner near the gravel driveway. I could see who was coming or going from my window.

Salmon and redwoods drove the local economy. Our neighbors were old timers, fishermen and loggers. They talked about arriving in Albion on horse and wagon. They wore OshKosh B'Gosh overalls and referred to cars as "machines". They were in tune with nature and gave me the knowledge of some of the old ways.

They taught me how to predict rain by watching the way birds fly. How to make soap from blue flowers. How to avoid a mean bull and not spook a flock of sheep. How to grow giant carrots by alternating gardens and letting the ground rest every other season.

Our peaceful country life was soon shattered. There was a mass exodus of hippies moving "back to the land". They were escaping the craziness of the city, describing it like a war zone. They called our tiny town Albion Nation. Mom welcomed the flower children like refugees seeking sanctuary. She let them stay on our land and use our house.

People moved onto our property and our family home became an informal commune. They built cabins, pitched teepees and slept in vehicles. One cabin was built on an old growth redwood stump with a ring of smaller living trees. The floor was the stump, the walls and windows were built in between living trees. That cabin was featured in several books.

Instead of barn-raising parties, we had dome-bending parties. The plywood was soaked with water to make it flexible and we all helped bend it. The geodesic domes were magical little half-circles in the forest. The triangle windows glowed at night like a jack-o-lantern with too many eyes.

Everything changed at home. My parents gave away the television and filled the house with books. We didn't shop for clothes in department stores anymore, we got used clothing from "free boxes". Our family stopped buying white bread, soda and prepackaged food. We ate brown rice, whole wheat bread and lentil soup. My original motivation for being an entrepreneur was to buy Hostess Cupcakes and Milky Way candy bars.

We went to concerts with rock bands. It was not unusual to see a naked person standing on their head or twenty people chanting in a group hug. Many people were on psychedelics. Us kids were warned which brownies and drinks to avoid. I didn't have a sense of what was normal, I took all the experiences in stride. Everyone was nice to me and I never had any trouble, except once.

We were at a party with marijuana-laced brownies and the host didn't make a clean batch for the kids. We were told we couldn't have brownies, but I had such a bad sweet tooth, I snuck some. Half a brownie was a dose and I ate four or five whole brownies. I was sick and disoriented for many hours. The experience left me with a fear of drugs and that protected me for many years.

Mom had music jam sessions at our house every Wednesday. Over time, it grew to what seemed like a hundred people playing instruments in our living room. There were some great musicians that came through there and I soaked in a lot of musicality.

Some nights there were dance parties and they played records. We had boxes of albums, an extensive collection of music, and I listened to every one of those albums. There were large catalogs of classical, world, folk, pop and jazz. But at late night parties they passed on the mellow records and played Jimi Hendrix, The Who, Rolling Stones, Frank Zappa, Miles Davis.

My parents had huge Voice Of The Theater speakers in our living room and they got cranked up. It was uncomfortably loud, even when I went to my room and shut the door. Sometimes I left the house to escape the noise. I walked far into the fields in the moonlight. Acres away, I could still hear every word of the songs.

Mom and I were driving to the Albion Store and picked up a guy who was hitchhiking. Albion was so small that everyone knew everyone else. This guy was called Crazy Charlie. There was white all the way around his pupils and it made his eyes look crazy, that's how he got his nickname.

He was standing with his thumb out, by the Azalea Acres sign. He was scruffy-looking with a small build, long messy hair and dirty clothes. He got in the back seat and rode to the store with us. He was very quiet and polite and made no unnecessary conversation. I glanced in the mirror of the visor and could see his intense eyes looking out the window. Many years later, I found out that Crazy Charlie was Charles Manson.

In third and fourth grade, I didn't attend public school. I went to a "free school", where the grown ups weren't teachers and there was no curriculum. Mom founded the private Headlands School and The Albion Community Center, which included an alternative school program. My education amounted to reading American Indian stories and learning how to use an abacus.

When I was eight, I learned to play guitar and sing songs. I memorized songs by songwriters such as Hank Williams, Bob Dylan, Joni Mitchell, Paul Simon. I asked my guitar teacher if I could write a song myself. He guided me to write a verse, fit the words to a melody and find chords that sounded good. Then he had me write a chorus and second verse the same way, and showed me how to stitch the parts together. That day, I became a songwriter and have written almost every day since.

My parents ended their marriage when I was too young to notice. They asked me how I felt about it and I said it was fine with me. But I didn't really have a concept of what was happening. Mom took us kids and went to live in Hawaii.

We camped on a coffee plantation, where Mom's friends lived in a small house. They grew lettuce to eat with avocados, instead of bread. There were plenty of avocados, bananas, coconuts and guavas, but I felt hungry all the time.

We went to Kona and slept on beaches in sleeping bags. The native Hawaiians weren't happy about sharing their island with us. From their perspective, they had been a state barely a decade and now their pristine beaches were being occupied by feral hippies from the main land. I didn't understand anything about the politics until years later.

Some of the Hawaiians were aggressive and dangerous. They asked to borrow our van and Mom innocently thought she was doing a favor for her "neighbors". They maliciously drove it off a cliff, leaving our family without a vehicle. One of Mom's friends, a young man named David, was sitting under a palm tree and was murdered for no reason. I knew it was serious, but I didn't really understand what was happening.

The violence convinced us to get off the beach, but it wasn't enough for us to leave the island. We went to stay on a Macadamia nut farm, where people were allowed to camp out in exchange for work. There was a community kitchen and one of the cooks had yellow eyes and yellow skin. Mom's eyes got yellow too. She went to the hospital with advanced hepatitis. She had complications and almost died.

Dad came to Hawaii and put us kids on a plane to relatives in Florida. I arrived in Miami with big knots in my hair and staph infections on my skin. I wasn't allowed to go in the pool, even though it was hot. I stayed inside with stinky medicine on my skin, while my cousins went swimming. Usually I loved visiting Florida, but this time I was miserable.

Eventually, Mom recovered and we all returned to Albion. Our home was still a disorganized commune. In hindsight, the chaos had a big impact on my emotional state. But at the time, I was still a kid and always found ways to have fun.

One of my favorite things to do was talk to interesting people who came to visit. They told amazing stories of their experiences. We didn't have television and some people were more fascinating than books. I aspired to live a life that would be full of interesting stories to tell.

One of these fascinating people was a man from England. He told stories of sailing across the ocean by himself, jumping trains across America, and kayaking on the Amazon River. He talked late into the night and I hung on every word of his adventure stories.

He lived in San Francisco and came up to visit once in awhile. One time, he showed up really late at night, almost dawn. He woke me up and was very agitated. He was talking strangely and said the entire county was going to be destroyed. He'd driven all the way from San Francisco to save me, because I was pure and innocent.

I was relieved when he left my bedroom, but soon he came back with a mug of hot tea. The cup was half-filled with sugar and the tea tasted like warm syrup. He told me to drink quickly and kept talking about how he was going to save me from destruction.

He was going to drive me to the city and put me on a plane. He said I could go anywhere I wanted. Did I want to go to

Hawaii? That would be a warm place, where I'd be comfortable if I had to sleep outside. He wouldn't go with me, he'd buy me a ticket and give me a little money.

After I drank the sweet tea, he told me to get up and put on my shoes and coat. It didn't feel right, but I didn't know how to disobey, because I was a child and he was an adult. I followed him outside and he said to get in his car. I told him I didn't want to go, but he started crying and saying he didn't want me to die. I finally got in the car to calm him down. I didn't know that getting in a car was the worst choice to make in a kidnapping situation. I foolishly thought I'd be able to jump out somewhere before we got to the highway.

He tried to start the car, but the engine wouldn't turn over. I silently prayed hard that it wouldn't start and it didn't. He was aggravated and flooded the engine. He said there was no time to waste and we would have to hitchhike to the city. I quickly got out of the car and took a few steps in the direction of the house. He didn't physically stop me. But he started crying, begging me to come with him and I did.

We walked for a couple of miles as the sun was rising. He kept saying Northern California would be destroyed within twenty-four hours. He talked about enemies, fake religions and nuclear bombs. He was going to fight, but he didn't expect to win. He was going to sacrifice his life, but he wanted to save mine.

A car drove up from behind us. He put his thumb out and the car stopped. He told me to get in the back and he got in the front seat and closed the door. I waved goodbye and took off running. I could hear him calling for me and then the car drove off. I glanced behind and saw him driving away. I kept running until I got home. Everyone in the house was still asleep.

Half an hour later, I heard him return and I hid in the basement. I heard his car start up and drive away. He was seen in San Francisco briefly and then disappeared. Several months later, his car was found in Mexico. To my knowledge, he was never seen again. I didn't know I'd escaped a kidnapping attempt. I just thought he was another weird grown up.

Five miles from our house was Azalea Acres. They were known for hosting an annual Hell's Angel party and we were warned to stay away. But the rest of the time, they were just regular locals. Sometimes they'd invite the neighbors to parties with local rock bands, like Cat Mother, who toured with Jimi Hendrix.

It was at one of those parties that I first observed the power of song. While the band was playing, the audience was ecstatically dancing. But as soon as the song ended, the crowd went back to talking and being ordinary. When another song started, the place became magical again. That was the day I recognized my calling. I was a songwriter. Songwriting was my vocation, it would be my lifework.

I was a child of the flower children, but I wasn't a "hippy". The Sixties influenced me, but I didn't have a say. The choices of an older generation were imposed on me. The positive aspect was growing up in an atmosphere of music, creativity and free-thinking. The negative part was the insecurity of being a child in a chaotic and dangerous environment.

# Chapter 3

# On The Backs Of Angels

I returned to public school in fifth grade, but I couldn't get into the swing of things after all the disruptions. No one noticed that I was troubled. I dropped out and it didn't seem to matter. I spent my days writing songs, playing piano and reading books. I hiked around in the woods for hours.

A man came to our house with a Shetland pony. He asked Mom if we could keep it for a while, because he had to move. We had a fenced field, a couple of acres with a little barn. The pony had thick, soft, golden brown fur with a blond mane and tail. Her name was Molly and she was the best thing that ever happened to me.

Every day, I spent hours riding and brushing my pony. When it was cold and rainy, I cooked oatmeal with pieces of apple and brought the warm mash out to the barn for her. I taught her tricks, like shaking hands and rolling over. Molly was my closest friend and therapy pet.

Several years later, the man showed up with a horse trailer. He said he had found a place for Molly and was taking her with him. I screamed and cried. It was no fair. He'd left her for years and she was mine now. I wouldn't let him take her away from me.

I ran out to the field and jumped on the pony bareback and started riding. But when the sun went down, there was nowhere to go and I went home. The man put Molly in the horse trailer and drove away. My heart broke and I was in a deep depression for a long time.

In seventh grade, I went back to public school. I was hoping that middle school would be more tolerable than elementary. Many days, I caught the school bus to town, but didn't go into the school. When the bus let us out, I slipped off-campus and out to the headlands. I climbed down the cliffs, where I couldn't be seen from the road by a truant officer, and found a comfortable rock. I spent the days singing, writing and reading. Sometimes I just sat quietly and looked at the ocean and sky. I attended less than half my classes and, in eighth grade, I dropped out again.

By this time, the wave of hippies coming from San Francisco had ended. Most of them left and only a few people were still living on our land. Those who stayed became neighbors and the pseudo-commune disappeared. We went back to being a nuclear family, sort of. Dad wasn't there anymore and I spent the rest of my childhood raised by a single mom.

Dad had another child, my half-brother, who grew up in Albion, a few miles from my house. Dad traveled and enlisted in the Air Force. He came to see us sometimes and occasionally we stayed with him on the base. We didn't visit much, but he made sure he always had extra bedrooms for us.

My early years were challenging and weird, but not worse than anyone else's. Everybody had to experience difficult times and many people survived much worse circumstances than mine. Overall, I was blessed and protected. I made it safely past many precarious perils.

I carried an image in my mind. I was stepping off a mountain, just about to tumble into a chasm. Angels flew up from under me, each bending its back so my foot was stepping on it. I walked across the abyss without falling. I walked on the backs of angels.

I was unharmed physically, but I did have to deal with emotional damage and suffered from recurring nightmares. In one persistent dream, I was running so fast I was flying. One foot pushed off the ground and I flew through the air a long distance before the other foot touched down. I was going incredibly fast, when suddenly there was an insurmountable wall in front of me. I couldn't stop in time or change directions. I slammed into the wall and woke up.

The running nightmare happened over and over, throughout my childhood and into my late twenties. Then one night, I had a lucid dream. I'd never heard of lucid dreaming, it just happened and I learned the term later. I was having the running nightmare and I saw the wall. I became conscious that I was dreaming and realized the wall existed only in my imagination.

All the other times I had the running dream, I always slammed into the wall and woke up. But this time I flew full-speed into it and didn't wake up. The wall wasn't brick and concrete. It was soft cardboard that broke into jigsaw puzzle pieces and floated away. Behind the puzzle was a residential street with flowers and lawns. I landed softly on my feet and walked down the sunny street. I never had the running dream again.

I had many recurring nightmares and feelings I didn't recognize as symptoms: emotional numbness, hyper-vigilance, social disconnection, depression, anxiety, severe introversion. I heard someone ask Mom if I was autistic. I thought he said artistic and was surprised when Mom said no, I wasn't.

As painfully shy as I was in conversation, I didn't have stage fright. People described me with words like talented, precocious and prodigy. I soaked in the attention and the complements gave me confidence. Performing was a way to get attention and compensate for the lack of supervision at home.

Being able to write songs allowed me to express myself when I was too shut down to talk. I learned later that severe shyness and sensitivity was a trait common to many songwriters. When it was difficult to think straight in a conversation, songwriting offered control over words.

Though I was shy, there was one person I was completely comfortable with and close to, my best friend Sophie. We played extravagant games of make-believe, drew art, baked chocolate chip cookies and talked about everything. We wrote songs to perform at her mom's church. I was thirteen-years-old when we wrote *King Of Kings*.

We were invited to perform the song at a missionary conference for several thousand people. It was the largest audience I'd ever performed for. The song organically became popular in praise and worship. It was translated into numerous languages. Over time, it was considered to be a classic, common in hymnals, and it earned a gold record for Petra.

In ninth grade, I was invited to be part of a new Alternative School on the high school campus. This was finally a program that worked for me. They allowed me a lot of freedom to choose my own curriculum and schedule, but also gave me enough structure to keep me engaged. I thrived and became a straight-A student.

I was asked to speak as a student representative at a statewide convention of K-12 teachers and administrators. I accompanied the superintendent, two school board members and the teachers who founded the Alternative School. We flew to San Diego and I had my own hotel room. We did a presentation called "Alternatives To Suspension: A Way In, Not A Way Out." I was the token drop-out who had become a model student.

Ever since elementary school, whenever I was actually attending school, I played in the band. My teacher was Mr. Ayres and he taught music to every grade, from kindergarten to high school. His class was the only part of the educational system I enjoyed. In high school, I played flute in the marching and concert band.

I was in a community orchestra, conducted by Mr. Ayres, and we performed classical music by Bach and other composers. Mrs. Ayres was a first and second grade teacher and I wrote a play with her class that the kids performed on television.

For several seasons, I was in the pit orchestra for The Gloriana Opera Company, performing operettas by Gilbert and Sullivan. I sang with a student rock band at proms and dances. I performed solo, singing cover songs and originals, playing anywhere I could.

I joined a judo club at my high school. I competed and won the lightweight girl's championship for Northern California. More than strength, I used visualizations that were taught to me by my judo teacher. I learned how my mind could influence my body.

When I pinned an opponent, I visualized that my spine was a steel rod. The steel went from my head, through my spine, and all the way down to the center of the earth. I focused on the image and it made me unmovable. When I pushed my opponent, my hand reached a hundred miles and that image made my touch more powerful. That visualization technique won the championship and helped me achieve goals throughout my life. It's the Bulldozer Effect.

Even though I had dropped out multiple times, I excelled in the Alternative School. I worked hard and was able to graduate a year early. My last year of high school, I got the lead in a musical theater production of *Carnival*. I was popular for the first time, which was disorienting. Cheerleaders and football players smiled at me in the halls, it was strange.

The day I graduated high school, I wore a white dress with lace and red flowers. I performed a piece by Debussy on a grand piano and got a standing ovation. When it came time to graduate, I put on a cap and gown and lined up. I stepped in time to *Pomp And Circumstance*. It was a strange feeling not to be sitting in the bandstand, playing the flute part, like I had for many other graduations.

I marched by a classmate who was my age. He jumped up and grabbed my arm, pulling me out of the line of graduates. He urgently whispered I was making a mistake and wasn't supposed to be graduating. We'd been in the same class since second grade and he knew how much school I skipped. It didn't seem possible that I was graduating a year before him. He thought I must be confused. It was funny, but understandable. I laughed and pulled my arm out of his grip. I continued down the aisle and up to the stage to get my diploma.

It was expected that I would go to college. Everyone in my family had a degree and a career. Since I graduated early, I decided to wait before applying for college. When someone offered me a job babysitting and a place to live in Jerusalem, I happily accepted. I wanted to get as far away from the small town as possible and see the world. Israel was literally "as far away as possible", almost halfway across the planet.

Dad was in the Air Force reserves and he got us free flights to England. After a day or two in London with Dad, we said goodbye to each other. I took off on my own for the first time in my life. I headed to the southern coast of England to see Albion, the namesake of my hometown. The steep cliffs looked liked home and I understood why it had been given the same name. It was funny leaving Albion and traveling thousands of miles to end up in Albion.

I spent a couple of days in Southern England and Wales, eating clotted cream and scones nearly every meal. Then I took the ferry to Ireland and leaned on the railing on the way over. A young man stationed himself beside me and offered me a cigarette. I said I didn't smoke. He lit up and talked and, when his cigarette was finished, he offered me another one. I said no thanks. He smoked and talked until it was finished and offered me another, I said no again. This repeated a few times until I finally accepted. A chronic chainsmoker wore me down and that's how I became a smoker.

In Dublin, I went to a pub. Nobody asked my age and I bought a pint of Guinness. It was so strong and thick, I could only take a few sips. Then an Irish man bought me another pint and put it beside mine. I protested because I had barely started the one I had. He laughed like I was joking. Someone else bought me another pint and another and another and eventually I had half a dozen pints of Guinness lined up in front of me. I still hadn't made it through half of the first one.

I was surrounded by a group of drunken happy locals, excited to meet a girl from California. They talked loudly, yelling out stories and jokes I couldn't understand. They sang beautiful Irish songs. A man climbed onto a table and stood on it, splashing beer and singing at the top of his lungs.

Later that night, a bomb blew up the train from Dublin to Belfast. I had intended to take that train in the morning and decided to continue with my plans. I figured they wouldn't be likely to bomb the same train twice in a row and I was right. I was right, but stupid and too young to take risk seriously. I headed innocently into a war zone.

Barbed wire fences surrounded downtown Belfast. Tanks were parked on the side of the street. There were guarded entrances into downtown. Soldiers, with machine guns and bulletproof vests, patted down anyone who wanted to go shopping or eat in a restaurant. There was a strict curfew and the city was completely empty at night.

I travelled through Scotland, Northern England and back to London. I got on a plane to Tel Aviv and went into another war zone, as though it wasn't a risky thing to do at all. I barely thought about it.

I spent six months in Jerusalem, babysitting and staying with friends. I lived in the Ultra-Orthodox neighborhood of Mayasharim. To be respectful and fit in, I wore long dresses and covered my head. Pushing the baby stroller, I looked indigenous and tourists snapped my photo. I attended a religious school, where I learned to read the Bible in the original Hebrew and Aramaic.

An ancient wall surrounded the old city of Jerusalem and, one afternoon, I climbed a carved stone stairway to the top. There was a path along the top of the wall, with look out slots where Biblical soldiers watched for enemies. A young man came up behind me and started talking to me in Arabic. He was trying to give me money. I later learned that, if I had taken his money, he would be legally allowed to assault me. But I pushed it away and the bill fell to the ground. He picked it up and tried to give it to me again. There was nobody else around and I was really scared.

I remembered a lesson at my judo club. A visiting teacher showed us where to push on a neck artery to choke someone. He said it would make them pass out and we'd have to let go or it would kill them. The technique wasn't allowed in competition, it was only for self-defense. The teacher wasn't supposed to be teaching it to high school students, but I'm thankful he did. I remembered the technique the first time I needed to defend myself.

I pushed my knuckle into the attacker's neck artery and locked my elbow. When he tried to approach me, his voice went up in pitch and he had to step back. It sounded funny and we both laughed. My knees were shaking, but the self-defense technique was working. Every time he pushed forward, my knuckle cut off the blood to his brain.

I was able to hold him off for a while. Another man ran up to us, shouting. He grabbed the attacker, pulled him away from me and restrained him. He spoke to me in Arabic, then Hebrew and, when he saw me struggling to understand, switched to English. He asked if I wanted to call the police. I had no experience with crime and didn't know the right thing to do. So I said not to call the police, I just wanted to go home. He pushed the attacker away, yelling at him in Arabic.

My rescuer was a well-mannered young man. He'd seen the attack from the ground and had run up the stairs to help. He escorted me down off the wall. He walked with me to a bus stop and waited until my bus came. I thanked him warmly and went home, shaken and upset.

At the house, I told my friends what happened. They gossiped on a phone call to the States and the rumor passed around. Mom was at a festival and overheard a conversation about a girl from Albion who was attacked in Jerusalem. In their version, I pushed a man off the Wailing Wall. Mom was shocked and upset. But all she could do was write a letter, because I didn't have a telephone.

Israel was at war, but I got used to it. Young people, my age and older, walked around with loaded machine guns. Soldiers were allowed to carry them off-duty, so they'd be ready if needed at a moment's notice. Streets were kept meticulously clean with no trashcans, so there would be no place to hide a bomb. The littlest piece of litter was handled by the military. Bombs were small enough to replace the lead of a pencil, carefully glued back together and dropped on a schoolyard.

The news reported a bomb had gone off, killing three people and injuring a dozen more. The bomb was concealed inside a piece of fruit and planted in a fruit stand at the market. I'd been shopping at that very market the day before.

My visa expired and the government offered me citizenship. In spite of war, I liked Jerusalem. It was an impressive city with amazing architecture and culture. But I didn't feel like I belonged there and I didn't want to serve in the army, which was a requirement of citizenship. I decided to head back to the States.

I found inexpensive seats on a cruise ship to Italy. The seats were on the bottom level, but I was allowed to go anywhere on the ship. The bottom level was next to the employee quarters. One of the employees was a young man, who invited me to drink Ouzo with the other workers. An hour later, he asked me to marry him and proposed again every day I was on the ship.

The Greek Islands were particularly beautiful, sunny in blue and white colors. When I got to Italy, I took the train to Paris. The city was fascinating and I loved the food and art. But I felt lonely and it kept raining. I bought a one-way ticket to New York City.

I lived in Brooklyn with a woman I'd met in Jerusalem. When her boyfriend wanted to sleep over, he gave me the key to his apartment. His place was full of pennies and he said I could have them, that I'd be doing him a favor if I cleaned them up.

Pennies were everywhere, in the bathtub, in jars, in the cabinets and drawers, on the floor. I was broke and scooped the pennies up gratefully. I could buy ten chicken wings for a hundred or catch a bus to a job interview for twenty. Talk about starting from the bottom.

I got a job at Kosher King, a specialty fast food restaurant. There was a Rabbi on staff full-time. He spent most of the hours reading holy books in the supply room. He came out once in awhile to bless the burgers and fries. I continued to write songs and perform, playing at Brooklyn College and local cafes.

I went to the library several times a week, where it was warm in the winter. I studied for the SAT test and applied to universities. I was accepted into several schools and chose University of California in Santa Barbara, because they offered majors in both playwriting and music. I was tired of the New York winter and the beach looked inviting.

When I arrived at the campus, the dean summoned me into his office. He said he was impressed with my application essay. Everyone in the office had read it because it was so creative. For my essay, I wrote a fictional story in italics and a traditional biographical essay in regular text. The fiction and the essay switched back and forth. The reason my application was so original was because I had no guidance and just made up what I thought would be an interesting story to read.

I met the dean again the following year, when I won the Sherrill C. Corwin Metropolitan Theater Playwriting Award for best one-act play. The name of my play was "On A Mobius Strip". It was about a man and a woman who have a conversation, but never connect.

I received a letter from the biggest Christian music publisher, Maranatha Music. They sent me a contract for the song *King Of Kings* with a five-figure check. It was an unimaginable amount of money for a teenager, and my co-writer Sophie got the same amount. When I filled out the contract, I didn't think my name Naomi Batya Ginsberg sounded like an artist. I dropped the last name and filled out the contract as Naomi Batya.

Nearly a decade later, the Christian rock band Petra recorded the song on their album *Petra Praise: The Rock Cries Out*. The album got to number two on the Billboard charts for best praise album. It was in the top ten album sales for Christian Contemporary for over a year. It earned a certified Gold Record and won a Dove Award.

I didn't hear about Petra's record at the time. The royalty checks increased, but nobody notified me about the success. I found out about it a dozen years later, when I looked up my name online. It was a strange feeling to learn I'd had more success than I thought I did.

At UCSB, student fees included health benefits and I decided to try counseling. I was having nightmares and felt moody and emotional. I thought it might be useful to get professional help. The therapist was a nice man and we talked for an hour. I don't know what we talked about, but I never opened up. I was accustomed to intelligent banter without revealing my feelings. He never scratched the surface of me. At the end of the hour, he said he didn't think I needed to see him again, but I could come back if I wanted to. I said I'd think about it and never went to therapy again.

I used the health benefits another time, when I got severe stomach cramps. I went to the clinic and the doctor was surprised to find out that I had a bleeding ulcer. He'd never seen anyone my age in that condition. He said it was probably caused by extreme stress and not eating often enough. He prescribed medicine and forbade me from alcohol and coffee. He recommended more frequent meals and a bland nourishing diet. I did as he said and improved in a few months.

Obviously, I didn't know how to take care of myself. It didn't help that I had developed the habit of being stoic. I didn't recognize how emotion was powerful enough to cause a bleeding ulcer. I didn't know my childhood was still affecting me, I really didn't think it was all that bad. Many people went through much worse experiences than I did. That way of thinking prevented me from addressing the source of the ulcer and other symptoms.

But I was having too much fun in college to think about anything that serious. I kept the past far in the distance and engaged myself with the present. The demons slept all day and came out in nightmares.

# Chapter 4

# The Music Business

I kept writing songs and performed twice a week in a café for tips and meals. I earned a small fee performing on the weekends with bands, sneaking into clubs with a fake ID. I also had a couple of part-time jobs at a cafeteria and a movie theater. I carried a full-time curriculum and enjoyed being a student.

As I was interested in scriptwriting, I attended a summer program at the American Conservatory Theater in San Francisco. The next summer I did a program at the Oregon

Shakespeare Festival in Ashland. I got a part as an extra in a Hollywood movie called *Marilyn: The Untold Story*.

All my classes were in music and theater. Other than an English class, I didn't take any of the requirements. Halfway through my sophomore year, I was told I had to take requirements and wouldn't be allowed to take any more electives. By then, I had already taken most of the classes that interested me. I was getting paying gigs and turning down tours to be in school. I decided to drop out of college and be a full-time musician.

Even though I had a history of dropping out, I was worried about telling my parents. My family was educated, Dad was a doctor and Mom was a social worker. My brothers were getting degrees in medicine, law and business. I assumed my parents would be disappointed in me, but they weren't. They gave me their blessing.

The only person who was upset that I was dropping out was my playwriting professor. He got angry with me and said I was wasting my gift. He said I was his star student. He believed I'd be able to write for professional theater and film. We stood in the courtyard for a while and then he wiped an angry tear from his eye. He wished me luck and walked away.

The professor was the only person who stood up to me. It was a form of caring I was not accustomed to. Maybe I should have listened to him, but I was driven to write songs and perform. The drive was fierce and had such a hold on me that I didn't even think I had a choice.

I was nineteen when I dropped out of college and moved to San Francisco. I played every chance I got, in clubs and recording sessions. I performed solo and gigged with numerous bands. It was a fun way of life and I was the center of the party. People surrounding me were excited about my musical abilities and made me feel valued.

I heard about a band that had a show and needed a bass player. I volunteered for the gig. I didn't know how to play bass, but my roommate had a bass and an amp she didn't use. Bass lines only had one note at a time, so how hard could it be? That was my thinking.

There was one guy who said women couldn't play bass. He said women played too soft and didn't rock. That's why bass players were always men. I took his words like a personal challenge and worked hard. That negative comment goaded me into becoming a professional bass player.

I learned how to make a grassroots living as a musician. For the first few years, the pay wasn't steady and I found jobs in between gigs. I'd get employment and then quit as soon as it conflicted with a tour. Most jobs only lasted a week or two. I was a bartender, prep cook, art salesman, and festival vendor. The worst job was assembling board games in a factory, breathing shrink-wrap plastic in a warehouse with no windows or air filters.

It was adjacent to being in the music industry when I got a job delivering singing telegrams. They gave me a company van to drive to shows. I used the back of the van as a dressing room to put on a giant rooster costume or an enormous teddy bear costume. I had a helium tank and blew up a dozen balloons. I surprised people and sang original songs that I wrote for each costume. I performed in mansions, conference rooms and birthday parties. I drove for hours between shows, all over the Bay Area.

I learned how to promote concerts. I could book myself with better pay than the club owners were offering. I put together shows at clubs and alternative venues, like

Sound Of Music and Valencia Tool & Die. I met Greg Perloff and did freelance work helping him promote shows for Bill Graham Presents. He went on to become one of the foremost promoters in the Bay Area.

Back when I signed my first publishing contract, I dropped my last name, but I still wasn't satisfied with the way it sounded. It was difficult for people to remember and pronounce. My band was writing a press release and I said I wanted to change my stage name. Someone suggested shortening my name from Naomi to Nomi, which was already my nickname. Someone else said to shorten Batya to Yah. Everyone started chanting it: Nomi Yah, Nomi Yah, Nomi Yah. The name stuck, some people even called me Nomiyah, like it was one word.

I found myself in the center of the early Eighties punk rock scene in San Francisco. I lived in the Mission District, a few blocks from Jello Biafra's house. I was friends with Dead Kennedys, Flipper, Michael Franti, Howie Klein, and many people who later became famous. I met touring bands like Meat Puppets, Husker Du, X, Dils, Siouxsie, New York Dolls.

There was a lot of drug use in the punk scene and, for a little while, I went along with the crowd. But friends were dying from overdose and suicide. In three years, I lost a dozen friends. I was at Biafra's house and some of the hardcore drug users were there. He started ranting at them about how stupid it was to do drugs. It struck me that here was someone I admired for his success in the music industry and he didn't touch drugs or drink. I saw a strong example of how to be sober and be the coolest person in the room.

When Biafra got married, I was invited to his wedding. The ceremony was in a cemetery on Halloween. He looked handsome in a top hat and tuxedo. He had a huge smile on his face the whole time. The bride was beautiful in a traditional white lacy gown with a long train.

The reception was in an old warehouse and Black Flag and Flipper played. The wedding cake had green frosting with bride and groom figurines in front of a tombstone. There wasn't any other food, except about one hundred boxes of cereal. No bowls or spoons or milk, just open cereal boxes. Fruit Loops, Cocoa Puffs, Lucky Charms, Cap'n Crunch. There was cereal was all over the floor, pulverizing under Doc Martins.

I was in a band with Jeff Miller, who later became famous as 4-way, lead singer of Bad

Posture. He bought us tickets to see Bob Marley in Jamaica. Sadly, Marley passed away before the concert. We wanted to go anyway, but didn't have the money for plane tickets.

My roommate was Barbara Klatt, an extraordinary artist who made intricate oil paintings. She said we could get a ride halfway to Jamaica with the Texas band MDC. They were friends of hers, on their first tour of California, and they were on their way back to Austin. We went to their show at the Mab, she introduced us and they agreed to give us a ride.

MDC had a white van covered in graffiti. It was full of equipment and packed with punk rockers. We drove down to a hardcore show in Los Angeles, where Henry Rollins did his first show as lead singer of Black Flag. I'd never seen a singer with so much raw power and energy.

The next day, we started driving east. We traveled through miles of flat desert and almost ran out of gas. We made it to a small gas station off the highway. The attendant was inside but, when he saw a group of punks climbing out of a graffiti-covered van, he locked the door and turned the open sign around to closed. We knocked and called out, but he went into a back room and didn't come out.

Across the street from the gas station, a man was sitting on his front porch. He got up and went into the house. Then he came back out holding a rifle and sat on the porch watching us. A sheriff drove up and got out with a rifle. He told us to leave town. We explained that we just needed gas, but he didn't care. He said to get out of his town immediately or he'd put us in jail.

We piled back in the van and left, with the police car escorting us until we were back on the freeway. I felt like we were in a B-movie horror film. I was afraid of what would happen if we ran out of gas. Fortunately, we were able to make it to the next gas station and on to Austin.

Jeff and I caught a bus to Miami and bought plane tickets to Jamaica. We met the original three singers of Black Uhuru on the plane. They were on their way to perform at Reggae Sunsplash. The concert was a memorial tribute to Bob Marley. Guest artists included Stevie Wonder, a young Ziggy Marley, The Wailers, Steel Pulse and many outstanding bands.

Eek-A-Mouse was there, performing his hit song *WaDoDem*. He was 6'6" and his song had the line "She too short and he too tall". As it happens, my travel partner Jeff was 6'9". Everywhere we went, Jamaicans sang that line to us. I never imagined that, years later, I'd be on tour with Eek-A-Mouse, playing that song every night.

When I got back to the Bay, Jello Biafra called. He wanted to know if some members of Black Flag could stay at our house. The band always stayed with him, but this time there wasn't enough room for everyone. Henry Rollins and a couple other people spent the night at my house. Henry seemed disappointed he wasn't chosen to stay at Biafra's house. He said it was because he was new to the band.

I gave Henry his first interview as a member of Black Flag. My roommate and I were the editors of Revolutionary Wanker, a punk magazine. We started it as a way to get into shows free. We'd been scamming, calling clubs and saying we were from Flipside, a punk magazine from L.A. We always got on the guest list, but lying felt bad and I worried about getting caught. So we started an actual magazine.

My roommate owned a magazine store called Burning Media and she had a lot of ideas. I was a writer and we got contributions from other writers and graphic artists. The magazine got us backstage and we interviewed performers.

We printed one issue on an anarchist printing press. It was in the basement of a house on Ashbury Street, a block up from Haight Street. Many years later, I moved into the house and didn't recognize it until I went into the basement and the press was still there.

We printed another issue of the magazine in a skyscraper downtown. A man was an executive by day and a punk by night. He snuck us in after midnight to use the copy machine. We printed 30,000 pages (60,000 counting both sides) until the machine broke.

The magazine grew into a really fun project, far beyond our original goal of getting on guest lists. We faked our way into becoming a real publication. Years later, the magazine became a cult-classic. It was displayed in an exhibit about early Eighties punk in the San Francisco Public Library.

The following year was 1982 and I heard rap for the first time. I'd been writing and performing lyrics without music that I called

"Rhythm Poems". Rap was the first time I heard anything similar. I was walking in the Fillmore district and *The Message* was blasting from an open window. I stopped on the sidewalk and listened intently to the whole song. My musical world exploded.

I immediately loved rap and resonated with it. I liked to think it was my nature, being born in the Bronx, birthplace of rap. I began booking rappers from New York, the only place there were rappers back then. I was the only promoter in San Francisco hosting rap shows, it was banned everywhere else. The other promoters seemed afraid of it. The rumors were that rap shows were dangerous, but I never had any problems. All the rappers were very nice and talented people. They didn't have turntables or backing tracks, just two microphones. One guy was rapping and another guy beatboxing. It was street corner music.

I moved into an apartment upstairs over Club Foot. The main promoter unfortunately committed suicide, so I pitched in to help with booking shows and managing the club. It was a small shabby nightclub in a warehouse district. It had a stage and a few folding chairs, basically an empty space. I put on shows a couple times a week. We sold snacks from a closet that was turned into a concession stand. Sometimes we got temporary permits to sell alcohol as a church. The shows were technically church events, I was ordained as a mail-order reverend and the tickets were donations.

Downstairs there was a rehearsal studio that we rented to bands. One of the bands was Silvertone, Chris Isaak's band before they were famous. Upstairs was a two-bedroom apartment where I lived with roommates. I booked a lot of shows and was able to pay musicians more than they made at many of the other venues. I kept expenses to a minimum and made ticket prices low enough to fill the club for every event. The bands split the door and the club kept the profit from concessions.

Next door to Club Foot was the clubhouse for the Hell's Angels San Francisco Chapter. They came to our shows and we visited their club. They were friendly and volunteered as security guards at our shows. They warned us to stay away from the clubhouse when there were biker parties, they wouldn't be able to guarantee our safety.

The Hell's Angels clubhouse was a large empty warehouse, ten times larger than our club. Right in the middle of the warehouse was a giant four-poster bed at an odd angle. There was hardly any other furniture, just motorcycles and parts scattered around. Sections of the walls were painted with intricately detailed artwork.

I had to get to a gig to play percussion with Mark Eitzel and The American Music Club. I packed a duffle bag with diverse percussion instruments, from a cowbell to a squeaky yellow rubber duck. I had to drop off rent to the landlord on the way to the gig. The rent was all cash and I didn't want to put the money in my purse in case I got robbed.

Club Foot was in a rough neighborhood, though I never had a problem. There was a police station a block to the north and the Hell's Angels a couple of door down. I knew the officers and the bikers, so I felt pretty safe. But I couldn't risk losing the rent money, so just in case, I put the cash in an envelope and hid it at the bottom of the duffle bag, underneath the instruments.

I didn't own a car, so I strapped the duffle bag securely across my torso and I went to the bus stop at the corner. After about ten minutes, a young man walked up and asked how long I'd been waiting for the bus. As I answered, he pulled a gun out of his pocket, then put it back in. I could see the shape of it through the fabric of his sweatshirt, pointing at me. He demanded that I give him my purse.

My knees started shaking. My thoughts raced to the rent money hidden in the duffel bag. I looked into his eyes for a split second to read who he was. He was a teenager, younger than me. He was a knucklehead, more of a reckless teen than a hardened murderer. I decided to talk my way out of losing my rent money. I did everything I wasn't supposed to do in a robbery situation. Staying alive should have been my priority. I did it all wrong and kept the angels busy.

I told him I had no money and took my wallet out of my purse. I opened it and showed him it was empty. He said to give him the duffle bag. I told him I was a musician on the way to a gig and opened the bag. I let him look inside and see the cheap percussion instruments, with the yellow rubber duck on top. I picked it up and squeaked it, an idiotic thing to do under the circumstances.

My heart was racing and my knees were knocking. Usually I was shy and quiet, but now I was nervously talking non-stop, as though he was less likely to shoot me in the middle of a sentence. I said I was a broke musician, waiting for the bus to get to a gig so I could get paid. All I had was three quarters to get a bus ticket. I opened my hand to show him.

The robber looked disappointed and sternly demanded I give him the seventy-five cents. I must have been temporarily insane, because I argued with him, gambling my life for under a dollar. I told him I needed the money to catch the bus so I could get to the gig. To my surprise, he pulled out a stolen book of bus transfers and gave me one. I handed him the quarters.

He ran away laughing loudly and jumped on a bus heading the opposite direction. My bus arrived and I went to pay the rent and play the gig, instead of going to the police station and filing a report.

I went on a short tour, playing half a dozen shows from San Francisco to Seattle. In Portland, I noticed a man in the audience relentlessly staring at me for the entire performance. I made a point of not looking at him directly, his intensity made me uncomfortable.

After the last song, I got offstage quickly. It was a small club, without a backstage, so I went straight to the bar. From the corner of my eye, I saw the man making a beeline toward me. I spotted the band manager, sitting at a table with some friends, and pulled up a chair.

I completely ignored the man, but I could see him in my peripheral vision. He sat on a barstool and stared at me. Finally he got up and came over to our table. He didn't look at me, but shook hands with the other band members and congratulated them on a great show. After talking and laughing for a while, he nonchalantly turned and started talking to me. He gave me a lot of compliments and seemed to be very stricken with me. He was trying to be flattering, but it felt creepy.

He showed up at our next three shows, following the tour and trying to get close to the band and to me. He said he was involved with a record label and dropped celebrity names. He wanted my phone number so he could sign me to the label, but I brushed him off.

I was glad when the tour was over, but the next day, I got a phone call from him. He'd gotten my number from the band manager by repeating the record label story. The manager had the idea he was doing me a favor by giving the stalker my phone number.

I got a number of calls and didn't answer. He left messages about how he was buying me a house. It was in escrow and he needed to make sure I liked it. Could I please call him back right away? He described the house in detail. He was going to buy a white grand piano and I would have a view of a lake while I played. I could live there and wouldn't have to pay for anything. I changed my phone number and didn't play with that band again.

I lived at Club Foot for a couple of years and put on a lot of great shows. But the building got sold, we were evicted and they turned it into a sewing factory. I was trying to figure out where to move, when I was offered a gig in Europe.

I spent six months in England and six months in Berlin. I composed and performed with an original theater production *Traumschuhe* (Dream Shoes). Berlin was having a record-breaking cold winter. Wind-chill got as low as sixty degrees below zero. A few days after the play wrapped up, I left quickly and went to Spain, where it was warm.

I got a gig playing bass in one of the most popular bands in Spain. The band was called Locura De Amor (Craziness Of Love). We played top-forty, reggae and alternative rock. Much of our set was original songs. During the summer and holidays, we played as many as eight shows a week.

I was living in a little cabin up on a hill. I walked home from town, climbing the ancient stone stairs that went up the steep mountain. Even though I was young, I had to keep stopping to catch my breath. I'd been smoking since I was seventeen, on the ferry to Ireland. It felt wrong to be in such bad health in my early twenties.

In addition to the health issue, I'd been noticing something about cigarettes that bothered me. If I was in a room and nobody was smoking, all I had to do was light up and several people would follow my lead. I felt guilty about being a bad influence.

I sat down on the steps to rest and a couple of people, who were much older than me, stepped around me and continued climbing at a quick pace. Halfway up that mountain, with a stunning view of the Mediterranean in sunset colors, I made a vow to quit smoking. I never had another cigarette.

I was in Barcelona and there was white liquid in all the gutters. I asked what was going on and found out about Chernobyl. The fallout fell on the grass, it was eaten by the cows, and now there was radiation in the milk. From Russia all the way to Spain, people were warned to not drink the milk. Instead of pouring it out in kitchen sinks, they brought the cartons outside and poured milk into the streets, as a symbol of protest and outrage.

My favorite gig in Spain was a seasonal event called Los Pirates (The Pirates), held on a remote beach. A boat, decorated like a pirate ship, docked in the harbor of the little town of Cadeques. It sailed the audience out to a remote beach. There was no other access to the beach, steep cliffs surrounded it. We hauled our music equipment out on the boat on Fridays and brought it back to town on Mondays, camping out on the beach for the whole weekend. Los Pirates operated every weekend for two months, during the busiest tourist season in the summer.

The boat picked up customers in town three times a day. Three groups of meals were prepared from the makeshift kitchen, grilling fish and serving alcohol. The staff dressed like pirates. There was a generator with lights strung up and an amplified stage. We played three shows a day, performing well into the night, for a total of nine shows in three days.

When the last boat went back to town, the band and staff camped out on the beach. The moon got so bright and the water was so clear, the stones on the bottom reflected the light and made the sea glow silver.

In the fall, the tourists left and we didn't have as many shows. I got a seasonal job picking olives. It didn't pay much, but I got bottles of the best stone-pressed olive oil in the world. The orchard was owned by twin brothers, who spent every night in the bar, getting drunk and talking about olives.

Every day, the twins provided lunch for the crew. We sat at a picnic table under the olive trees. They grilled fresh fish and opened bottles of Spanish red wine. Sourdough bread was drizzled with olive oil and topped with garlic and tomatoes. The lunch had a few simple ingredients, but it was delicious to the point of beating out the best restaurants in the world. The sun was warm and the turquoise waves of the Mediterranean splashed on the shore. It was a wonderful romantic life.

I lived in Europe for a couple of years. I loved Spain, but I missed the U.S.A., where everything was familiar, where I belonged, where I got the jokes. I was tired of having a language barrier. I was fairly fluent and even wrote songs in Spanish. But I missed subtlety, nuance and slang.

I returned to California and worked in the Bay Area as a music producer. I had my own studio when home studios were rare. I learned how to use recording equipment when I was in Spain. A band member had a studio and I spent all my free time learning. I bought a portable, multi-track, recording rig. I carried it in a suitcase and provided a mobile recording service. I put up flyers at shows and music stores. Artists hired me to record their concerts and demos.

I released a couple of albums of original songs. I performed solo, played in bands and worked as a studio musician. I composed and played music with the dance troupe Contraband and the street theater group "TAG" (Theater Action Group). I performed at a fundraiser hosted by Elizabeth Taylor.

For several summers, I performed at the Oregon Country Fair. I played flute in the marching band and we were in a parade that wound all the way through the fair, twice a day. After the parade, I was in the orchestra for the Karamazov Brothers circus act. It was the only professional gig in my life where I had to read music.

I put on the ambitious RadCultFest (Radical Culture Festival). The festival featured over one hundred performances. There were bands, theater productions, dancers, poets, films and performance arts. The festival took place over ten days and events were scattered in more than forty venues, throughout the city and the East Bay.

One night, I was invited to a bonfire on the beach in San Francisco. It turned out to be the first Burning Man festival. There were a couple dozen people there and many of them were on psychedelics. The following year, I was invited again, but I didn't go. Parties with drugs weren't my scene. Nobody had any idea what Burning Man would become later on.

Wherever I went in the world, I could play professionally. It wasn't easy, but it wasn't hard either. I used the Bulldozer Effect over and over, pushing myself towards success. I made good money and had few expenses. For years at a time, I toured so much I didn't pay rent or have a car. I visited family and friends when I wasn't on the road. On tour, food was provided, I got per diem pay, someone always bought drinks, the band bought clothes for me to wear onstage. My income was pretty good and I had very few expenses, the combination made me feel rich.

I was in my twenties and making a living playing music full-time. I had worked hard and succeeded on my own terms. I felt pretty good about myself.

# Chapter 5

# My Family

Performing professionally never made me an extrovert. I was shy off-stage and didn't feel like I belonged anywhere. I was comfortable with a small number of close friends, on the road with the band or having an intimate conversation with a friend. But most of the time I felt alone, especially in a crowd.

In my professional life, I was the opposite. I flirted with the audience, smiling and dancing. I wore eye-catching fashion, flaunting bare legs and high heels. I hung out at the bar and let fans buy me shots of whisky and ask me for stories about the tour. Making it in the music industry required using everything I could bring to the table. I did what was expected from me as a woman entertainer. But as soon as the show was over, I left the clubs quickly.

In my personal life, I had a couple of boyfriends over the years. But I didn't get serious with anyone. I was moving around too much. I wanted to stay on the road and not get too attached. I also didn't want to deal with jealousy issues. Many of the musicians I knew had problems with their partners being suspicious. It was understandable though, because there were temptations all around and many of the musicians were cheating.

When I saw a band member cheat, I wasn't allowed to say anything, even if their wife was my good friend. I was under a strict code of silence. If I broke the code, and talked about what I saw, I would lose my job. I was already an exception, being allowed into the "boys club" of the music industry. I could be easily kicked out.

Personally, I was too introverted to cheat. Being close to one person at a time was quite enough for me. Most of the time, I stayed in hotel rooms by myself. I liked having time to write and practice.

My attitude about staying single completely changed. It happened instantly, the moment I saw my future husband for the first time. When he walked into the room, it was like a grey world was struck by lightning and turned to rainbows.

We had friends in common and they had invited him to come to a party. I was in between tours and subletting at a country property, not far from Mendocino. It was a big piece of land, with a river running through the center and a hanging footbridge. It had been a hippy commune called Oz in the Sixties. By the time I was there, the commune was over but it was still called Oz. The main house and cabins were rented out separately.

There was a party at the big house. I was in the living room, playing a song on guitar. The door opened and my future husband came in. I looked up and it was love at first sight. We talked all night, sitting around a fire by the river.

Everything about him rang true and fascinated me. I had never felt like this before. I felt a deep pool of kindness and goodness in his core. We were very different, but we had the same worldview. I resonated with him when I learned he was a refugee, since my mom and grandpa were refugees. We got along smoothly and fell in love.

He went back to Santa Cruz, where he lived. We communicated and met, and got to know each other for the next few months. The sublet at Oz was over and I was in San Francisco, housesitting an apartment for a few days. He came to visit and we went together to Haight Street, where he had an appointment.

I found a café, where I could wait for his appointment to be finished, and ordered a cappuccino. The barista made the drink and handed it to me. I gave her a twenty-dollar bill and she opened the cash register to make change. I looked down into the cup and saw strange little objects in the white foam. I looked up and a chandelier was swinging back and forth, dropping little chunks of the ceiling into my cappuccino.

I asked the employee if that was an earthquake. She said she didn't know, she had just moved to California and never been in an earthquake. She looked worried and I reassured her that earthquakes are no big deal, she'd get used to them. I asked for a refund, since there was sheetrock in the cappuccino. She was still holding the twenty-dollar bill and she handed it back to me.

I turned around and saw a young mother running outside in a panic, leaving a toddler alone in the café. The young child was about to start crying and I leaned down and spoke calmly to her "Let's go find your mommy". I gently took the child's hand and walked with her toward the door. The mother ran back into the cafe with fear on her face. She thanked me, picked up her child and ran back out.

I was laughing to myself about how tourists couldn't handle a little earthquake. I walked outside and saw a chimney had fallen and crushed a car. Then I realized this was bigger than I thought. Someone was blasting the breaking news on a car radio. The Bay Bridge broke and freeways were crushed. Sixty-seven people died. The World Series game was cancelled. It was a magnitude 6.9.

Hundreds of aftershocks drove masses of people out of their houses. Everyone camped in parks, where nothing would fall on them. We sat on a hill in Dolores Park all night, with thousands of other people. The power was out all over San Francisco, except at the hospital and the U.S. Mint. The Marina District was on fire and glowing brightly in the dark city.

It was a sleepless night and we discussed getting out of the city. The road south to Santa Cruz was closed, so we went north over the Golden Gate Bridge. Mom had moved to

Berkeley and rented out the house in Albion, but she kept a vacation cabin on the property. We got up to Albion and stayed there for about a week.

When the road to Santa Cruz was finally back open, we drove down. We parked downtown and walked, arriving at the exact moment the historic brick Cooper House was being demolished. It had been dangerously cracked in the earthquake. There was a big crowd and the mayor said a few words. Then they imploded it with loud bangs and the bricks fell down.

We heard of a caretaking opportunity. An acquaintance had a rental house that was vacant. It was in an area that was hard hit by the earthquake, but his house was not damaged. When he built the house, he put in a very deep foundation and the structure was heavily retrofitted.

Even though his property was not affected by the quake, it was surrounded on all sides by houses damaged beyond repair. The whole street was a red-tag zone. Landlords were prohibited from renting to tenants until after inspection, and that could take six months to a year. The owner didn't want the house to be empty, so he offered it to us free of rent.

All of our neighbors had left their houses and there were a lot of abandoned cats. I bought big bags of cat food and that was my small contribution to earthquake relief. I was heartily thanked by cat owners, when they came back to find their pets well-fed and healthy.

After we were together for nearly two years, we got married. The ceremony on the beach was performed by a rabbinical student, whose father was one of the scientists who won the Nobel Prize for the Big Bang Theory. The only other person there was one friend as a witness. After years of working onstage, I didn't want my personal life to be the center of attention. I wasn't one of those women who dreamed about a big wedding, I was the opposite.

When family and friends found out we got married without telling them, they felt hurt. So we threw a big party and invited everyone. We had almost no money, but we scraped together a few hundred dollars. We rented an off-season Boy Scout camp for the weekend, including a lodge with a kitchen and a few cabins. Our friends cooked, since we couldn't afford catering.

Dad showed up with a six-foot long loaf of braided challah tied to the roof of his car. Mom drove down with a close friend of the family. My theater friends performed with giant puppets on stilts. They built a bride puppet with a long trailing veil. It was a beautiful sight to see the giant bride walking in the forest. My musician friends set up on a stage in the lodge and played late into the night.

I gave bass lessons to my husband and formed the band YahWanag (Jah Lion). Everyone in the band took turns being lead singer and writing songs. We had four members from the four directions, North and South America, East and West Africa. Three of us lived together, which gave us a lot of time to practice and write.

Our band got popular and made a good living, attracting talent scouts and label interest. Grocery store workers and restaurant waiters gave us free food because they were fans. All of our shows sold out.

It was my idea to split the net five ways. Each of the four members got a fifth and whoever secured the gig got a fifth. We'd sit around a table late after a show, counting out cash, like dealing cards in a poker game with five players. I hustled and got us a lot of shows, so I frequently got paid double.

As the band was becoming successful, I had shoulder-length dreadlocks. Then I got pregnant and it made my hair grow so long the locks touched the back of my knees. I kept performing for the next eight months because I needed the income, but it wasn't easy. The cigarette smoke in the clubs made me nauseous. I felt the baby kicking to the music like he was dancing, which made it hard to breathe. When I couldn't take a big enough breath to sing anymore, I quit performing.

I had a home birth and it was an unusually long and grueling labor. Contractions started on Saturday morning and lasted until Tuesday afternoon. I suffered cramps for seventy-six hours without food or sleep. It was more painful than anything I could have imagined.

The moment my son was born, it was the most joyful feeling in the world. What I thought was love and happiness turned out to be poor substitutes, like comparing a light bulb to the sun. His skin was soft and had no blemishes. His eyes were pale and got darker every day. He had a full head of black curly hair in tiny locks. He smelled like a bouquet from heaven.

My life permanently changed for the better. I wanted to be there full-time and experience every second with my baby. Everything about him delighted me. I was troubled when we were separated. I quit the band and stopped performing for a few years.

A few months of blissful motherhood had passed when we got bad news. It was a big loss when Grandpa passed away. He led an inspirational life and had a delightful intellect.

He kept his word and left me a small sum of money and stocks. I kept my word and set out to buy my first property. I had $25,000 for a down payment. I had no credit, good or bad, and no consistent employment records. Fortunately, the banks were willing to be flexible back then. They only asked to see a year of utility bills paid on time. I was approved for a loan of $65,000.

The real estate agent told me I couldn't afford a livable house for that amount anywhere in Santa Cruz County. But I found something half an hour from town in the mountains.

The house was a cute two-bedroom A-frame cabin with a big loft. It had a large deck next to a creek and a quaint footbridge to the road. Over half a century before, San Francisco Chronicle had a promotion and gave away all the lots on our road. If someone paid for a one-year subscription, they got a deed for a vacation property. Their attitude was the land was worthless, after logging it to make newspapers. People came in the summer to camp out and eventually built cabins.

We lived there for over a year. Then one winter night, there was a landslide on a neighbor's property above our cabin. Dozens of trees and tons of earth fell down, demolishing the footbridge and crushing our Toyota Landcruiser. The noise woke me up and the baby was crying. I went over to the crib and picked him up. At that moment, a tree crashed into the house.

It was frightening, but we got out safely, carefully climbing over downed electric lines. It was raining and dark. We had to ford our way across the rushing creek. We spent the night with a kind neighbor. In the morning, we saw the wreckage.

The tree that hit our house fell in the landslide and, as it was falling across the creek, it hit an electric wire. The top of the tree snapped off, about fifteen feet of it. If the tree hadn't broke where it did, the end of the tree would have gone straight through the house, where I was standing holding the baby. Instead, it broke the exact amount, so that it touched the roof, leaving only a tiny repair to patch. The tree slid down against the front window of the living room, touching the window but not breaking the glass. We were blessed that nobody was hurt. I was interviewed on the evening news.

We repaired the damage from the falling trees and put the house on the market. We'd been planning to move to town anyway. My son was starting preschool and we wanted to reduce the driving. I liked the idea of living in town and not having to deal with falling trees and rising rivers.

In the short time we lived in the house, the property values went up. Our net profit was $50,000. My credit had been established with timely payments on the mortgage and I was preapproved for $150,000. Our real estate agent insisted we still couldn't afford to live in town. I didn't accept that and managed to find a nice house on my own for $187,000. The property had fallen out of escrow, but the sellers had already moved. They were desperate to sell and we got a good deal.

The carpet smelled like dogs, but when it was removed, there was pristine hardwood floor underneath. All around the house were piles of junk that we hauled to the dump, revealing a beautiful big backyard. After a coat of paint on the walls, we had a lovely home. It was in a quiet neighborhood, a few blocks from the ocean. Every summer on the weekend, we could hear bands performing at the Santa Cruz Beach Boardwalk, in the concert series. The elementary school and preschool were walking distance.

I needed a job, but I wasn't really qualified for anything. I wanted to find an occupation where I could bring my son. He was too young for preschool and I didn't want to leave him with a babysitter. The whole point of giving up the music industry was to be with him. My husband and I tried being vendors at music festivals, selling crafts and cooking Ethiopian food. But it was better to be onstage than be a vendor.

I found a sign on a bulletin board. It was an ad for a job as a private chef. I applied and got the job cooking for a wealthy couple with a child. They lived in a large ranch house on top of a hill and welcomed my son coming with me to work.

Twice a week, I shopped and cooked for them at their house, making multiple meals for them to heat up. I also prepped ingredients, put each in a separate container and labeled it. That made it easy for them to cook something from scratch, without having to shop or clean or cut.

They each had requirements and I catered to every request. For example, the woman only ate tomatoes if they were raw, the man only ate tomatoes if they were cooked, and the child didn't eat tomatoes at all. I cooked separate meals for each person.

About six months after I started cooking for them, the couple bought a mansion. It was a massive, twenty-five thousand square foot house. There was a gym, a spa with a waterfall, a pool and a deck. Each of the three wings had a living room and kitchen. It was on top of a mountain with a view in every direction.

The famous owner of a major software company built the mansion with a futuristic computer system. The heating, air conditioning, lights and music were programmed separately in every room from one central computer, which was unheard of at that time. There was an extravagant theater room, with a screen that descended from the ceiling and surround sound speakers built into the walls.

My son watched cartoons on the big theater screen and played with the little girl when she got home from school. Her room was full of every toy and game imaginable. She had a giant tricycle that she rode down the long hall between her bedroom and her parents' bedroom. On my breaks, I took the kids swimming in the pool or the hot tub.

I cooked in the kitchen in the main wing. It had state of the art everything. The appliances and cookware were all of the highest quality. There were two refrigerators, three ovens and four sinks. There was a large pantry, with room for everything to be stored neatly in cupboards. I had always loved to cook and invent recipes, but this kitchen was beyond my wildest dreams.

I prepared meals for distinguished guests. Some of the guests I cooked for were John and Caroline Kennedy (who later died in a plane crash), Thomas Dolby (who invented Dolby Sound), and John Robbins (heir to Baskin-Robbins Ice Cream).

I was making a living and it was fun to spend time in a mansion. But it wasn't my mansion. I was a house servant and I felt uncomfortable in that role. At night, after I put my son to sleep, I drove to a nearby community college and studied accounting. I figured I could learn bookkeeping and work from a home computer.

I continued cooking twice a week, but also worked part-time doing bookkeeping. I worked for a CPA during tax season. He gave me stacks of paper to process and mentored me. I didn't want a full-time job until my son was in elementary school, so I took a series of small bookkeeping jobs.

A restaurant hired me to help them reduce employee fraud. I set up a system of financial accountability to track funds from waiters to cashiers to managers. I established a paper and computer trail that eliminated the problem of embezzlement.

A local drum factory heard about my work at the restaurant and hired me. They built handmade drums distributed in Guitar Centers nationwide. They had a big problem with employee theft. I developed a system of serial numbers that tracked the product, from creation to shipping to point of sale.

The people I cooked for invested in a local music club called Palookaville. They knew I had a music background and did bookkeeping, so they offered me a job in the nightclub's office. I was thankful and excited for the opportunity. It was a perfect position, where I'd be able to work in the music industry during school hours. I wouldn't have to work at night or go on tour.

I went to the club for my first day of work. It was a classy nightclub, in the heart of downtown. It had a stage on one side and a bar on the other side. There were stairs that went up to a mezzanine and some offices. The owner was waiting to meet me, he was very warm and I liked him right away.

He showed me to my office, but it wasn't upstairs where the other offices were. Instead we went to a door backstage and up onto the stage itself. He led me behind the backdrop curtain to a ladder and we climbed up to a small loft. It was directly over the stage, with a view of the whole club.

The loft was equipped with a desk, a chair and filing cabinets. When my family got an adorable Basenji puppy, I brought her to work with me and carried her up to the loft. She curled up on my lap and slept while I worked.

At work, everyone was talking about David Nadel, a promoter at the Berkeley club

Ashkenaz. He was shot by a customer and died. Years later, I became one of a series of promoters who took over running the club. Another decade after that, the night manager was also shot by a customer, but he thankfully survived.

Eventually I moved from the loft over the stage to the nice offices off the mezzanine. I did bookkeeping and other administrative tasks and was in charge of all the documents, from financial to artist files. We promoted many great concerts, the most memorable being Johnny Cash. I continued working in the club until a few years later, when the business changed hands and they let everyone go.

Of all the jobs I ever had, Palookaville was my favorite. I was disappointed to have to start over again. I liked the office environment and the predictable schedule. I liked the orderliness of the files and the teamwork of being part of a staff. I applied for a job at University of California Santa Cruz and was accepted.

I became the Financial Assistant to the Dean of Student Affairs. I worked on the beautiful campus, ten minutes from my house. I designed a database to track work-study funds for each financial aid student. I enjoyed designing databases and filing systems. The way that files belonged in a file cabinet, the way accounting fit into categories, was like the art of fitting lyrics to melody and rhythm. When it was all perfectly organized and everything fit, it was satisfying.

My car broke down and it wasn't worth fixing. I'd always driven used beaters that cost under $1,200. I'd drive one for a few years until it broke down, then get another one. This time I had a good job and had $2,500 to budget for a car. But it was difficult to find a car worth buying at that price and I couldn't afford a monthly car payment.

After several days of searching for a decent used car that I could afford, I got home and found an envelope from my publisher. I opened it and there was a royalty check for $13,000. I bought the best car I could afford. It was a brand new Toyota Corolla and I paid cash for it. It wasn't a flashy vehicle, but it always made me feel like a rock star. How many songwriters can say they paid for a car with a single royalty check? That car is still running.

We saved up enough so we could travel to Ethiopia to see my husband's family. He hadn't seen them for twenty years, since he'd left as a refugee. They were excited to meet our son for the first time. My mother-in-law didn't mind our interracial interfaith marriage, but she was upset my husband had married outside the tribe. She made the best of it by declaring me an honorary tribe member. After her announcement, she gave me a hug and accepted me into the family.

We went out for a walk and I heard my voice blasting out into the streets of Addis Ababa. It was surreal, an incongruous juxtaposition of worlds. A local record store had got ahold of my album and was playing it for their customers. We went inside and the owner of the record store was thrilled to meet me in person, apparently my reputation preceded me.

I met a woman who was born in Jamaica and repatriated to Africa as a child. She wrote a book about her experiences and was trying to get it published. Numerous publishers had rejected it. She wanted my advice and showed me the manuscript. It was a pile of scraps of paper with scrawling handwriting. She could barely afford a pen and paper, much less a typewriter or computer.

She asked if I could take the manuscript and type it and help get it published. I explained I was in the music business and didn't know anything about book publishing. But she begged and I couldn't say no. I took the manuscript and a bunch of her photographs and brought them back to America. For a couple of years, I got letters from her with revisions and additions. The book became *Living In Shashemane: A Memoir Of Repatriation* by Anne Marie Hamilton. It was the first book on the subject of repatriation that was written by someone who had experienced it first-hand.

I liked the routine and the calm office environment of the university job. The steady paycheck and benefits were a welcome change. As much as I enjoyed and had a knack for computers, that path was suddenly shut to me. My hand started hurting, it felt like my wrist was on fire. I kept going to work, but within a couple of days, I could no longer use my right hand at all. I had to stop working and go into physical therapy.

The university made extraordinary allowances, providing health care and hand therapy. They brought in ergonomic experts to give me a very expensive chair and a special keyboard and mouse. But after six months, I still wasn't able to use my hand and I became unemployed again. The university had generous benefits, training me on voice command computers, so I could have alternate employment. But voice command was not very good at the time and it was frustrating.

Unemployment benefits ran out and once again I didn't know how I would make a living. I couldn't hold a pen in my right hand or use a computer. As a writer, I felt disabled, scrawling lyrics with my unskilled left hand. I was very worried I might lose the ability to play piano. After taking a break for a few months, I was relieved to find that playing was actually a healing movement that alleviated pain.

I decided to do the same thing I always did. It always seemed to be the easiest thing to do. I went back to performing music. I quickly found enough work and joined a number of bands, specializing in reggae, hip-hop and dancehall.

Local gigging often required driving for many hours. It was much harder than touring, because I didn't have a driver. I would get home early in the morning, in time to wake up my son, make him breakfast and take him to school. I was driving home, when I fell asleep and woke up on the wrong side of the road. I had to pull over and sleep in the car.

I knew how to make a living playing music. But I didn't know how to do that with a family. I was burning the candle at both ends and my marriage suffered. My husband didn't want me to continue performing, it wasn't easy being married to a professional musician. After ten years, my marriage collapsed. Faced with the choice, I picked music over marriage.

Maybe we didn't handle it the right way. We just did what all good parents do, we did the best we could. I got full custody and we went to Berkeley to live with Mom temporarily.

# Chapter 6

# On Tour

I got a call late one night, offering me four gigs with reggae star Eek-A-Mouse. I would have to get to Oregon in time for a show the next day. My friend said she'd drive with me, her son and mine were best friends. She was a professional singer and we sometimes helped each other with childcare.

We left at dawn and drove all day. Between us, we scrounged up a couple of Eek-A-Mouse albums and listened on the trip up to Oregon. I wasn't familiar with his music, other than the hit *WaDoDem* that people had sung to me in Jamaica.

By the time we got to the club, it was late and the opening bands had already played. My friend dropped me off and took the kids to get dinner. The place was packed. I went backstage and there was Mouse, towering over everyone, while the band members, three Caribbean men, stared at me doubtfully. A Jewish woman was not a likely-looking reggae musician, but I was used to not fitting in.

There was no time to get to know the band, because five minutes later, we were walking onstage. The bass player tossed me a set list. I faked my way through the show. I didn't know any of the keyboard lines that are so distinctive in reggae. But I played in time and mostly in the right key, and the audience didn't seem to notice. The band shot looks at me when I messed up, which was every song. But Mouse liked my stage presence and thanked me after the show.

We played three nights in Seattle. Then I collected my pay and said goodbye to the band. I was about to head home, when Mouse pulled me aside, where the rest of the band couldn't hear. He asked if I would be willing to continue on tour. He would buy me a plane ticket to Los Angeles and we'd play a few gigs in Southern California. Then we would leave the rest of the band behind and fly across country, to tour with his East Coast band.

When he told me the weekly pay, I immediately said yes. As a single mom with no child support, I needed the income. I didn't know how I was going to handle it, but it was a great opportunity I couldn't pass up. I spent the next few days lining up a series of friends and relatives to watch my son. I sent him to stay with his grandparents and flew to Los Angeles for an epic tour.

My music career was peaking, but at the same time I missed my son every second. I cried every day like a baby. I ran up more than seven-hundred dollars a month, talking to him on my cell phone, before unlimited plans existed. I was trying to make up for not being there in person, full of guilt and separation anxiety. I bought presents in every town, whenever we stopped for gas or stayed near a store. It was emotionally wrenching, feeling so much pain and, at the same time, feeling the gratifying high of performing at a top level.

I deserved the success and I had to make a living. I had worked countless thousands of hours, practicing and writing every day for twenty-five years. I worked on holidays and weekends, when everyone else was having fun.

I ran a few miles each day to handle the athletic demands of performing long concerts. Finally all the work was paying off. I felt regret that my son wasn't with me, but I was doing the best I could.

We played a few sold out shows in Los Angeles. The band was happy that I had learned the keyboard lines. We played a couple more shows in San Diego. Then Mouse and I got on a plane and flew across country, to meet up with his East Coast band.

The new band was different, younger with a hip-hop swagger that I liked better than traditional reggae. The tour was supporting the *Black Cowboy* album. We went to a western wear store and Mouse bought us outfits and cowboy hats to wear onstage. My boots had bullet bootstraps, that were later confiscated by airlines security. They made me take the bullets out.

We toured the East Coast and the South, stopping to play shows almost every night. We headlined at festivals and clubs and drew packed crowds everywhere we played. I wasn't a fan of Eek-A-Mouse before, but touring with him, I grew to appreciate his skills. Everyone in the band was talented and we locked in musically, developing arrangements until we were really slamming. Audiences responded enthusiastically.

I was at the height of my performance ability. I could distinguish nuances of time and play around a beat, instead of directly on it. Slightly ahead of the beat, the music was hot and exciting and could make people dance. Slightly behind, it was cool and relaxing and could make them listen. My hands were so responsive they could find any note instantly. Sometimes I observed my fingers flying over the keys, like they knew what to do and were part of the music, without any thought or effort from me.

We checked out of a hotel in Richmond, Virginia. The tour bus wouldn't start and it was towed to an auto repair shop. We were standing in the parking lot with all our equipment. Mouse was on the phone to the booking agent. The hotel manager came out and she asked if we needed help. We explained that we had to get to a show in Baltimore. She said her husband was a limousine driver. Mouse hired the driver to bring us to Baltimore. The driver stayed on tour with us until the tour bus was repaired. He drove us to Philadelphia, New York City, Hartford and Boston.

It made me feel like a celebrity pulling up to a club or hotel in a limousine. But after a couple of days, my opinion of limos changed. It began to feel like an uncomfortable car where I had to sit sideways or backwards. The low ceiling and dark windows felt like a hearse, not a luxury vehicle, and I was glad when we were back on the tour bus.

We were invited to headline at a festival in an Indian casino near San Diego. They paid us very well to get off the tour for one gig. They bought five first-class tickets, but there were seven of us, since the East Coast band had two back up singers. By the time they realized they needed to buy two more tickets, there were no more seats available in first class. They bought two coach tickets and Mouse and I sat in coach. He said he wanted the rest of the band to sit in first class because they were all from ghettos and it would mean a lot to them.

Actually, I had never flown first class either, but I didn't say anything. I appreciated Mouse giving up his right, as lead singer, to take the better seat and it wasn't easy for him to squeeze his large frame into coach. While the band members ordered drinks in first class, we sat in the back of the plane and wrote a song. The song was called *Prison* and ended up on his next album *Eeksperience*. When the record came out, he played our song at every show, often starting the concert with it.

When we landed in San Diego, we had a day to rest before the gig at the casino. Mouse's family lived in San Diego and he didn't stay with us in the hotel. The next afternoon, the casino sent a limousine to pick us up. Mouse was supposed to meet us, but nobody knew where he was. We stood around the parking lot for over an hour. The driver got impatient and left to use a payphone. The band didn't mind waiting. Most of them had never been to California before. The weather was amazing and the beach was right next to us.

While we were waiting, two helicopters came and hovered overhead. Suddenly I heard gunshots. Nobody else seemed to notice. I interrupted the conversation and asked if anyone had heard the gunshots. They laughed at me, thinking I was joking or paranoid. They had experience with crime on the streets of New York, but they didn't expect guns at the beach in Cali.

I knew what I had heard and walked out to the sidewalk to look down the street. A few doors down, two policemen were pointing guns at a man on the ground. They had shot him and he wasn't moving. He was a large black man wearing cowboy boots. I gasped for air. It was Mouse! He was shot! I started running toward him. But when I got closer, I saw it wasn't him. Relief poured over me.

It was bizarre to see a tall black man in cowboy boots, at the exact time and place we were waiting for Mouse on the Black Cowboy tour. But this man was much thinner and had different hair. I later heard on the news that he robbed a liquor store and was killed by the police.

My heart was pounding and I tried to calm down. As upset as I was, it was worse for the rest of the band. Everyone was black, except me, and they understandably felt threatened being in the vicinity of white policemen who had shot a black person. We were thankful when the limo driver returned and said he was taking us to the show. He'd located Mouse and someone else was picking him up.

We drove almost to the border of Mexico and got off the highway. For half an hour, we travelled on gravel roads. We got to a gate, a security guard opened it and we turned onto the reservation. We drove a mile down a long dirt road, the limo wasn't equipped for the bumps and it was uncomfortable.

We got to the outdoor concert. I was expecting to play in a fancy casino. But this was just a large flimsy-looking stage, built in the desert. The stage was brightly lit, everything else was dark and I couldn't tell how many people were there.

We pulled up to a trailer and were ushered inside. It was set up for us with snacks and drinks. The promoter was worried, where was Mouse, why wasn't he in the limo with us. Our driver assured him that he was in another vehicle and they were on their way.

The promoter was tensely talking about the situation at the concert. There were around forty thousand people in the audience. They'd been in the sun all day, drinking alcohol. Only security guards were allowed on the reservation, no police. People were getting drunk and volatile. Several fights had been broken up already. The audience had been waiting for Eek-A-Mouse for over two hours. They were restless and getting drunker. The promoter had been hyping them up to see our band all day and they were rowdy and impatient.

The promoter told us to get on stage, even though Mouse wasn't there yet. He asked us to play a few songs and maybe the audience would calm down. We were used to singing a few songs, warming up for Mouse, and said it was no problem. He warned us if there was any trouble, we should go straight to the trailer and guards would protect us. The way he was talking made me worried. I was scared, but didn't show it and neither did anyone else in the band.

The promoter led us, like soldiers in his command, to the side of the stage. He wouldn't get on stage to introduce us. He said the crowd was tired of him and had thrown beer cans the last few times he'd made announcements. He waved at me to go on first. I climbed up the metal ladder and stepped onto the rickety stage.

The spotlight was blinding, but I could see a few hundred people crowded next to the stage. From the darkness came a roaring rumble of conversation, shouting and laughter. Even though I couldn't see them, this was the biggest audience I'd ever had. I crossed the stage to get to the keyboard.

When I got to the middle of the stage, the crowd suddenly got quiet. I felt thousands of eyes turn to look at me. The rest of the band was hanging at the back and I was alone in the spotlight. The promoter had put me in this position by pushing me to go on first.

I could feel the energy of the crowd surging toward me. I grabbed that intimidating ball of attention and turned straight toward it. I boldly strode to the microphone in front of the stage. I didn't have time to think of what to say, so I went with a predictable cliché.

I lifted both my arms in the air and shouted loudly, pausing after every syllable. "Hey! San Diego! How are you feeling?" A huge cheer went up, a dusty drunken wall of sound. I felt a jolt of energy shooting through me. I shouted and waved my arms, whipping up the applause.

I turned and walked back to my instrument, relieved to hide behind the keyboard stand. The keyboard was already turned on and I tested a couple of notes. The audience responded to the sound enthusiastically. The band was almost ready, but the attention of the crowd was still focused on me. So I did one of my signature moves.

I leaped straight up into the air with my fingers stretched out in position and came down, playing a chord. Then I jumped back up and came down with another chord. Up and down I went, as I played a few bars of *WaDoDem*. The audience loved it and the cheering was deafening.

The back up singers came out and took the pressure off me. It felt like they had taken forever, but it was only a couple of minutes. The spotlight made time stop. The drummer counted off with his sticks and we went through a few songs. I looked over where Mouse should have been waiting to come out and begin the set. The promoter was standing there, gesturing for us to stretch it out.

We did some more songs. We sounded great and the backup singers helped a lot. But the fans had waited all day to hear Eek-A-Mouse. No matter how good we played, they hadn't come to see us. They bought tickets to hear Eek-A-Mouse.

They crowd got angry and loud, a couple of beer cans were thrown onto the stage. It felt like a punk concert, with all the jostling and pushing. The stage was swaying a little. I was afraid it might collapse. I glanced around for where I would jump off and save myself.

All the while, I kept performing and putting on a show. I smiled at everyone I could see in the light. I projected my energy far into the distance, waving at all the people I couldn't see. I'd had plenty of experience pretending like nothing was wrong.

Suddenly the crowd exploded, it sounded like a bomb went off. Mouse was climbing up the ladder and strolling onto the stage. He took his time strutting to the microphone. He tamed the audience immediately and held them captive for almost two hours. The wild crowd turned to putty in his hands. They were smiling and dancing under clouds of marijuana smoke.

After the show, we went backstage to the trailer. Three armed security guards stood outside the door. The crowd cleared out and we were driven to the chief's residence. They catered a dinner for us. We stayed all night playing pool, drinking top-shelf Scotch and smoking Cubans. The walls were full of pictures of the chief with presidents and kings, movie stars and famous musicians. The chief with Michael Jackson. The chief with Frank Sinatra. The chief with Ronald Reagan.

In the morning, we drove back to San Diego. It had been a very intense twenty-four hours with no sleep and we crashed at the hotel. The next day, we got on a plane and went back to the East Coast to continue the tour. Mouse and I sat in coach and wrote another song.

We performed almost every day, traveling up the East Coast and then West across the country. We were booked in Martha's Vineyard the same day that John and Caroline Kennedy went down in a plane. I had cooked for them in California and several years later, on the other side of the country, I was only a few miles from them when they crashed.

We were stuck in a traffic jam for over an hour. As we crawled forward, we got to an overpass and a man was sitting on the ledge. Police officers were talking to him. The man made a move, like he was about to jump, and the police grabbed him. They pulled him off the ledge.

One time, we drove through a wildfire. There was fire on both sides of the highway. I begged the driver to turn around. But he said we had to get to a gig and kept driving through the wildfire. We made it to the show on time and the driver looked smug. But I was angry with him, he didn't have the right to risk my life. Another time we were driving on a snowy mountain and the tour bus was slipping on ice. The driver put our lives at risk again.

The fans were warm and gracious to us, but some got pretty crazy. Salt Lake City was the wildest. People were excessively drinking and openly shooting up hard drugs. Women threw themselves indecently at the musicians. I was surprised at the underbelly of this ultra-religious society.

At one show, Mouse pulled about ten women up onto the stage. Then a swarm of people jumped up on the stage until it was packed with a hundred dancing fans. I held my keyboard with my left hand to keep it from being bumped off the stand, while I kept playing with my right hand. Mouse walked backstage followed by dozens of fans. The bouncers freaked out and started yelling at everyone, pushing people off the stage. The audience loved the crazy energy and started chanting Eek-A-Mouse, Eek-A-Mouse, until he came back and did a few more songs.

Whenever Mouse wanted an encore, he sang every song except his hit and left the stage. Audiences couldn't stand not hearing the hit and always cheered for an encore. He could get a crowd to chant his name or toss big buds onto the stage for him. He was a master of showmanship and timing.

There were often tall people at our shows. They came out to see the tallest reggae star. We met many famous football and basketball athletes. Some retired NFL players invited us to their house for dinner. They were so big they made Mouse look like a child. Their large living room felt like a miniature dollhouse filled with giants.

I met up with my son in California and was ecstatic to see him. I hugged him tightly and covered him with kisses. I gave him a duffle bag full of presents that I'd bought all over the country. I brought him with me on the West Coast leg of the tour. I couldn't stand being separated from him anymore and he was on summer break.

I didn't want him to ride in the tour bus because I didn't trust the driver. Plus I wanted to shield him from the drinking, smoking and bad language. I drove my own car. It was exhausting to drive all day and perform all night. But it was worth it to be with my son. It made me feel at peace to be near him.

Sometimes Mouse came with us in my car. After a lifetime on tour, he preferred driving in a private vehicle. In Washington, he bought a small cooler and a whole fresh fish. He squeezed the cooler under his large legs in my little Corolla, the car I bought with one royalty check. After a few hours, fishy water spilled onto the carpet. Mouse gave me money to get it detailed, but the new car smell never came back. He sure knew how to cook salt fish though, the best I ever had. He could prepare it without a kitchen, just a camp stove in a hotel room.

My son seemed happy being with the band. Everyone adored him and he loved the attention. Drunk, young women tried to hug and kiss him, he got irritated when I dragged him away. I didn't trust leaving him backstage, where people drank and did drugs during the show. I'd find a chair and put it offstage where I could keep an eye on him. He had video games and snacks to occupy him for the hour or so I was performing.

We were at a big sold out show at the Roxy on the Sunset Strip in Hollywood. I set up his chair behind a curtain, but he didn't stay there like he was supposed to. He stood in front of the curtain and started dancing. He was wearing an Eek-A-Mouse tee shirt with a matching headband and new sneakers. He had some cool hip-hop dance moves. The audience went crazy, taking his picture and cheering him on. He got caught up in the attention and moved closer to the front of the stage.

He got all the way to center stage, right next to Mouse. He totally stole the show. Mouse stopped singing and glared at me. I left the keyboard in the middle of the song and went over to get my son. I tried to make it look like part of the show, but it wasn't easy because he threw a tantrum. I took his arm and led him behind the curtain. He was fuming at me for interrupting "his" show and embarrassing him. He was seven-years-old and didn't understand this was my job.

I didn't know how to tour and be a single mom. It wasn't working and didn't feel right. I kept asking when the tour would be over. I was trying to figure out how to deal with the tour schedule and still be home in time for the beginning of the school year. But Mouse never answered, he always changed the subject. I finally realized he couldn't answer the question because the tour was never over. We had tickets to fly to Houston. We were touring the South and back up the East Coast. After that, there was a tour being booked for Europe and after that, Asia.

We were in San Diego and I was driving behind the tour bus to the airport. My mind was racing as we parked and walked to the gate. There was a plane ticket for me, but not for my son. No one was there to take care of him and I'd used up all my favors. Mouse said my son was welcome to come if I bought an extra ticket.

Rejecting opportunity went against a lifetime of being a reliable musician, of putting music first. But ultimately it all came down to one simple truth. There would always be another show to play, but my son only had one mother and I only had one child. He needed me and I needed him.

Mouse said the plane was boarding soon and asked what I was going to do. I told him I was getting off the tour, as long as he could find another keyboard player. He scowled at me and said he could get musicians anywhere in the world. He looked angry and sad.

I said goodbye to the band and took my son's hand. Mouse's anger melted and he gave us a hug, he understood why I had to stay. The band walked off in one direction and we walked in the other. A weight lifted off me and I knew I was making the right choice. I felt lighter and happier with each step.

While I was on tour, Mom and my stepfather found us a place to live called the Eco-House. I liked the way it rhymed with Eek-A-Mouse. It was a little bungalow close to school and Mom's house. The Eco-House was part of my stepfather's project developing three community gardens and a bike path. They needed a caretaker to live there for a year or two while they raised funds and worked on plans. It was wonderful to have that haven as a place to reboot.

The Eco-House was going to be an ecological demonstration museum. Construction companies donated time and materials to have their work featured. They put in bamboo flooring and counters because bamboo is a renewable resource. They refinished the cabinets to demonstrate reuse.

There was a job opening for the general manager of Ashkenaz Music And Dance Community Center. The club was walking distance from my house. I applied for the job and was hired based on my experience performing and promoting. I was given a six-month trial period.

The job paid for twenty hours a week, but I worked sixty or more. I was responsible for booking, marketing and operations. I was in charge of performers, employees and night managers. I gave regular reports at board meetings. They informed me that their existing audience-base was older and white and that they hired me to bring in diversity.

I began to book hip-hop, reggae and salsa every week. Right away there was a noticeable increase in the diversity of the audience. I kept a detailed financial record of each day and compared it to last year and the year before that, going back twenty-five years. Nearly every show, I broke the record in attendance and revenue.

I rearranged the existing schedule to make room for more diverse acts. There were some regular events that didn't bring in much money, but occupied weekly slots on critical nights. They'd been grandfathered in and I was careful to make allowances for seniority and not ax anyone completely. But I had to move things around and managed to ruffle some feathers of board members who were in those bands. They didn't appreciate being bumped to a less desirable night or being booked twice a month instead of once a week. I didn't pay attention to politics. I was trying to make the venue successful and achieve the goals I'd been hired to accomplish.

The day before the end of my six-month trial period, I was suddenly asked to step down. They didn't give any reasons and I could have made adjustments, but they didn't give me an opportunity. They already secretly hired someone else. My replacement was a white man, so much for increasing diversity.

Losing a job, while being the sole provider for my family, was stressful. I returned to performing and got steady work. I played local gigs three or four times a week. I made a meager living, but it wasn't easy to get by without touring, local gigs didn't pay as well. I moved my son's bed into my room and rented out the second bedroom to another single mom. I didn't like having a roommate, but I had to do what I had to do. I continued to have recurring nightmares, often about being in a hotel or trying to get to a hotel or trying to leave a hotel.

My ex-husband and I sold our house in Santa Cruz. We'd been there only a few years, but we'd bought it for a good price and market values had gone up. We were able to net a profit that we split between us. I took my share and put a down payment on a home in Oakland. It was an old-fashioned house built in 1921 with a lot of original details that made it charming. It was walking distance to Lake Merritt, but the neighborhood was a little rough and there were bars on the windows.

The house needed a lot of repairs and updates. I put in a new roof, retrofitted the foundation and upgraded the electricity. I replaced the furnace and the water heater. I built a one-bedroom apartment with a separate entrance by walling off an existing breakfast nook and half bath, and building an addition. I had to cut corners and hire a series of handymen, trading studio time for some of the labor. When it was finished, the apartment became a steady source of income, which was a welcome relief.

I continued performing in the Bay Area, but found it challenging to drive for so many hours. I had a home studio, before they were widespread, and started producing hip-hop and reggae tracks. I earned extra income and got credits on albums. I made tracks for an advertising company that made commercials for Comcast. I had songs placed in films and television shows.

Late one night, I was sleeping when the phone rang. It was a producer from Aftermath Records, Eminem's label. He was in town looking for songs for a new artist. But he was leaving early in the morning to go back to L.A. Someone had recommended me as a songwriter and he asked me to sing something for him. I was lying in bed with the lights out, singing a few of my songs into the phone.

I passed the "audition" because he said he'd like to take some songs back to the label, if I could get a CD to him by 9:00 am. I got up, went into my studio, and stayed up all night, writing and recording. In the morning, we met in a parking lot in Oakland and I gave him three songs on a CD. He listened while he was driving to L.A. Later that night, he called to say he wanted to sign all three songs to Aftermath.

I was offered a short tour with a reggae band. The shows were in Cabo San Lucas, Mexico. They put us up in a beautiful hotel on the beach. We performed at Sammy Hagar's Cabo Wabo Club for two nights. We were interviewed on Cabo Mil Radio station and they played a few songs from my album.

We performed at a huge festival for over one hundred thousand people. It was only a few months after the attack of September 11$^{th}$ and I'd written a song about the tragedy. I spoke in Spanish and dedicated the song to the three hundred and twenty-nine Mexicans who lost their lives in the attacks. A huge cheer went up at an unbelievable volume.

When I was singing, people held up lighters and sang the chorus with me. The sound of thousands of people singing my song was so powerful it brought tears to my eyes.

After the show, there were thousands of people in a line waiting to meet us for autographs. Many people thanked me for acknowledging the Mexican victims, who were completely unmentioned by American media.

When I came back from Mexico, I sat myself down and gave myself a good long talking to. It was time to give myself a slap in the face and have a come-to-Jesus moment. I had to stop going back to music and touring. I was a single mom and needed to be at home.

Music had always been my direction and focus. I had the drive to make it in the music business. I used a bulldozer approach, like Grandpa had modeled in his achievements. Drive was the secret behind making it in the industry. Talent was a factor, but drive was imperative. Drive put in the hours of practice and travel. Drive made relationships bend to its will.

But what was my drive for? What more was I hoping to achieve? I had toured the world. I had earned a gold record. I had sung an original song for an audience of one hundred thousand. Yes, I could get more success, but what for? I had something more important than my music career now and had to learn to stop being so driven. I was determined to really quit performing this time.

This was my only chance to experience being a mom. I wanted to go to every Little League game and take vacations to Disneyland. I wanted to have sleepovers and birthday parties. I wanted to see my son wake up on Saturday morning, turn on cartoons and eat pancakes. I didn't want to miss a single thing.

Offers to perform and tour kept coming in. I went cold turkey and sold my keyboard so I had an excuse to not take the gigs. It didn't help much though, because they were usually willing find a keyboard for me. The only thing I could do was say no, I had to turn down gigs, something I had never done before. I had to go against my nature. It was like I had always spun clockwise and now had to spin counterclockwise.

Although I continued to perform my songs once in awhile, when I stopped performing professionally I never went back to it. It was the end of one career and the beginning of a new unknown life. I didn't know what I was going to do. I'd recreated myself before, but as a single mom the stakes were so much higher. I held on to the example

Grandpa had set, to succeed in spite of obstacles. I held on to the Bulldozer Effect.

# Chapter 7

# Document Organizer

I was starting over, trying to figure out a life where music was not the primary goal. My objective now was to provide an income where I could work around my son's schedule. I applied to several jobs a day, but didn't get hired. As glamorous as it seemed, being a musician didn't look good on a resume.

I couldn't work computer-based jobs because the wrist pain continued. I went out for many hours a day, looking for work. Every day I was rejected. It was demoralizing.

I finally got hired at a deli. It was new and hadn't opened yet. The owner needed to hire a whole staff. I cooked and served and learned every element of the job. I helped set up menus, recipes, schedules, filing systems, employee records. I was overachieving because I wanted to become irreplaceable.

It was humbling, working a service job after being a musician. I'd been well-paid for performing in front of thousands of fans. Now I earned minimum wage, making sandwiches. But I wasn't too proud to earn a living.

The deli owner told me to change my schedule. She wanted me to start at 6:00 am instead of 9:00 am. I explained I needed to bring my son to school before work. There was no other employee who had a child, so I thought it was a reasonable request that someone else take the early shift. She said I could bring my son into work with me and he could sit in the back for three hours every morning before school. I wasn't going to do that and she fired me. Several months later, the deli went out of business, so the way I was treated wasn't the only bad decision the owner made.

I'd been an ideal employee, always on time, going above and beyond. Being fired as a single mom, with no child support, was very stressful. It was frightening how quickly I was facing poverty. I put on a brave face for my son and tried not to let him see the pressure on me.

I made a decision to never look for another job. I would be a business owner like Grandpa. I'd control my own income. I'd set my own schedule. I would never beg for a low paid job again, I'd tried that and it wasn't working. That was not for me, that was not who I was.

I sold some music equipment to survive and desperately searched for an idea for a business. The idea came while visiting the home of a highly educated, wealthy couple. The couple had a perfectly clean house, but a messy office. The desk was covered with disorganized papers. The floor was cluttered with cardboard banker boxes, stuffed full of documents.

It occurred to me that someone who could afford a house-cleaner, might be willing to pay for an office organizer. There must be large numbers of people in the same position as this couple, accomplished successful people without enough time for office work.

I had enough office experience to have the skills I would need. I researched to see what the competition was. I could only find a few professional organizers and no document specialists.

I went to bookstores and the library, reading dozens of books and online articles in a few days. I was thankful for the speed-reading class I took in high school. I studied filing systems, office organization and document retention.

I discussed my business idea with a few close friends and family. Nearly everyone said it was not a good idea. Paper was outdated. If there was no competition, it meant there was no demand for the service. People wouldn't be comfortable having me handle their private documents. What if I made a mistake, there was too much liability.

I considered the advice, but didn't let it stop me. When I went into the music business, they said it was impossible. When I bought real estate, they said it was unattainable. Maybe people only meant to protect me by warning me not to take a risk. Maybe they couldn't imagine creating something from nothing.

But I believed in my idea. I believed I could find enough small businesses and individuals who needed my help. Mom was one of the only people who supported me. She said it was a brilliant business model, filling a need that wasn't being met. She talked to her friends and helped me get my first clients.

I named the business Document Organizer and printed business cards and flyers. I took out a few inexpensive ads in school and temple newsletters. I made cold-calls to accountants, lawyers and case managers. Within a few weeks, I had enough clients to make a living. Soon I didn't do any more outreach and got all my clients by referral. From the first day, Document Organizer paid three times what I was getting from the deli where I'd been fired. My income later grew to be five times higher.

I ran Document Organizer for fourteen years, with a wide range of fascinating clients. I successfully facilitated multiple audits and court trials, going to the IRS and court as a professional witness providing documentation. I regularly saved clients money by finding unpaid property taxes, un-deposited checks, and forgotten envelopes of cash. Sometimes my services were purchased as gift certificates for birthday presents and Christmas stockings, often by a member of the family who wanted a home office straightened up.

Sorting documents was like a jigsaw puzzle or lyrics, everything had to fit. I developed a customizable system for filing documents that was simple and logical. Financial information was standard and everybody had the same system. The interesting part was working with someone's unique business, when I didn't know anything about it. Information could only be organized with an understanding of the subject. It was intriguing to delve into such diverse subjects as law, real estate, religion and science. As an outsider, I was able to see an overview and categorize the details.

The customized system literally mapped every single document they owned and applied to books and digital files too. It was so logical I could find everything quickly. I'd often get a call from a client frantically looking for a document and was able to tell them where to find it over the phone. I enjoyed hearing their sounds of amazement and sighs of relief.

My clients were interesting, successful people who fascinated me and made the work enjoyable. One client was an award-winning spectroscopist. I had to file thousands of lab reports and learn scientific words about experiments to prevent mold in peanut farming and other obscure subjects. I had clients who were real estate developers, agents and landlords. I learned a lot about real estate by handling their files. An attorney hired me to sort through forty years of banker boxes from a business that manufactured and installed garage doors.

One of my clients had a manufacturing company that made shipping containers. They customized them for military use, from portable housing to simulated cities for combat training. The filing system had to correlate with the computer organization and I had to learn to read military codes, government bid documents and architectural drawings. I designed and implemented a filing system and then taught their employees how to use it.

My most notable clients were Daniel and Patricia Ellsberg. Dan was famous for leaking the Pentagon Papers in 1971. I was his executive assistant for thirteen years, working with him in his office two or three times a week. I didn't know who he was when I started working for him. Becoming friends with the Ellsbergs, and the remarkable people in their circle, was a bonus I couldn't have foreseen when I started the business.

Dan saved large quantities of documents over sixty years. But this was not the clutter I'd seen in some offices. The majority of these papers were valuable historical archives. To organize them, I learned a great deal about history and politics. I was finally getting the higher education I'd missed, between skipping school and dropping out.

In addition to organizing documents, I was also Dan's executive assistant. I took care of travel and finances. I helped with research for his book *Doomsday Machine*, his writing for articles, and his speaking engagements. I provided documentation for the film *Most Dangerous Man In America*, which was nominated for an Oscar and won an Emmy.

I coordinated with Amblin Entertainment in the production of Steven Spielberg's movie *The Post*, starring Meryl Streep and Tom Hanks. The film was about the Pentagon Papers and Dan was played by Matthew Rhys. It got Oscar and Golden Globe nominations.

I found a dusty cassette of a private concert by Barbara Streisand and Marvin Hamlisch. They were performing at a fundraiser for the Ellsberg legal defense fund in 1973. I brought the precious recording into my studio and was honored to digitize it. Through the noise of the ancient cassette tape, Streisand's voice was amazing. I'd never listened to her before and became a fan of her vocal ability.

Everyone in the family was sad when my stepfather got sick and passed away. Karl was a wonderful person and it was a loss for the whole community. Mom wanted to keep living alone, even though she had an illness that made it progressively more difficult to walk and she had to use a wheelchair.

Mom left her hairdryer plugged in and it shorted the outdated outlet. The bedroom caught fire and it was especially scary for her because she was disabled. I offered to live with her, but she wanted to keep her independence. I suggested we sell our houses and buy a duplex. But she didn't want to move, she wanted me to move. I told her I couldn't afford a house in Berkeley and she offered to get a loan in her name and help with the down payment.

The real estate market was rocketing in the Bay Area and the in-law unit I added made the house in Oakland more valuable. It sold for $220,000 more than I purchased it for a few years before. I was flipping houses in slow motion.

I bought a house in Berkeley. It was walking distance to Mom's house. I got a good deal on it because it was a manufactured house and the neighborhood was run down. The house itself was a beautiful upscale home with skylights and hardwood floors. It was only three-years-old and didn't need any repair. It was nice to be in a house that didn't need work, for a change.

After awhile, I couldn't resist adding an in-law unit, since it had done so well in Oakland. I converted the garage to an apartment. It was my first time having a nice two-car garage with an automatic door and I didn't want to lose the luxury. But the unit brought in around $1,800 a month in rent and I wouldn't have paid that much to park my car.

I started dating a well-known music producer and composer. We'd known each other for nearly ten years. I'd been in recording sessions at his studio and we'd co-written songs. He was recently divorced and asked me out. After many years of being single, it was nice to have someone to do things with.

He took me to a restaurant in Sausalito with a beautiful view of the city. There was a full moon and the water and boats were glowing. He pulled out a diamond ring and proposed. The waiter popped a bottle of champagne, it was classic. We got married on November 11, 2011. We could never forget our anniversary because it was 11/11/11.

I continued working part-time in the music industry. I ran a songwriter competition at the Freight and Salvage for fourteen years with the West Coast Songwriters. I worked for their annual conference and founded a lyric contest. I got placements on television and albums. A song I worked on *A Man First* was on the compilation *Made In Amerika,* featuring Snoop Dogg. I invented a songwriting method I called Syllablizing, a technique of organizing lyrics onto a grid.

I co-founded the company Song Brigade for music publishing and artist development. I coached and co-wrote with talented young songwriters. It felt good to help aspiring artists with their careers, performance skills and songwriting. I knew I had spent too much time without direction and missed many opportunities. Often I wasn't able to recognize which choice was best to achieve my goals. Most of the time I didn't even have clear goals. I liked being able to give guidance and co-write with upcoming artists.

I was struggling financially even with three businesses: Document Organizer, the music business and being a landlord. I took an overview of the situation to see what I could improve. Document Organizer was a good business and I was successful. But it was a time-in money-out service company. If I didn't work, I didn't get paid. I could hire employees, but I knew that would create more work for me and increase expenses.

Document Organizer was providing half my income. The other half was coming from renting the in-law unit in my converted garage. Music income trickled in from songwriting, music production and artist coaching. But since I stopped touring, the income was unreliable. I thought of it more as a bonus than dependable cash flow.

Real estate had been dramatically more profitable than any business or job I'd ever had. It provided the most amount of income for the least amount of effort. Real estate was clearly the best business of the three from a financial standpoint. I calculated that if I had a few more units, I'd raise my income and be able to discontinue Document Organizer.

I didn't know how I was going to be able to buy a second property. I brainstormed how to achieve my goal. Grandpa had given me a few thousand dollars of stock in his will. The family's financial advisor was managing it. Over the years, whenever I made a little extra money, I sent it to the financial advisor to deposit to my account. I lived frugally and socked away every penny I could and finally got the balance up to a little over $20,000.

After the global economic crash, my account dropped to $16,000. The financial advisor reassured me to stay the course. She said it was "just a paper loss" and it didn't count if I didn't sell. She said the market historically always corrected itself. When my account dropped to $14,000 she repeated her advice, reassuring me not to panic. I took her word for it, I assumed she knew a lot more than I did about managing finances. She was an expert and other members of my family trusted her, so I felt confident. I got busy and forgot about it for a while.

The next time I checked the balance, it was a little over $3,000. I felt bitterly disappointed and offended. The efforts of my Grandpa and my own hard work had disappeared into thin air. I withdrew what was left and closed the account. I couldn't believe what kind of a stupid business this stock market was. The advisor kept getting paid and I lost the little that I had scrimped and saved. Maybe $17,000 was a small loss for the advisor's wealthy clients, but it was everything to me.

It was a painful and expensive lesson about trusting experts. I wish I could say that it was the only time I had to learn that lesson. But unfortunately it wasn't the first or last time. A bank screwed me over was when I was an eleven-year-old child. Grandpa gave me ten American Buffalo dollar coins. He said they were valuable and not to be spent. So I took the coins to Bank of America in Mendocino, where I had a savings account with a few dollars in it. I deposited it proudly.

I learned later that the teller didn't do me any favors. He deposited ten dollars into my account, without informing me that I would never get those coins back. He was just doing his job, after all I was the one who asked to make a deposit. But he could have been a better person and advised me not to deposit the coins. I was a child and thought the bank would safeguard my coins. Today that ten dollar deposit would have been worth nearly three thousand dollars.

I kept trying to come up with a way to buy property. My credit score was over eight hundred and I had little debt, but I couldn't qualify for a loan. After the financial crash, self-employed people were having trouble qualifying for mortgages. That's where I was stuck. The banks wouldn't count any of my income, except the net of Document Organizer. After deducting expenses, the net wasn't high enough to qualify for a bank loan.

The banks didn't count royalties as income. They disqualified rent income because the unit was attached to my residence. My tenant was considered to be a roommate who was sharing expenses, not business income. They weren't swayed by years of tax returns showing the rental as a business. It didn't matter that it was a completely separate unit with no shared space.

In hindsight, this was an early indicator that there was a big opportunity for private lending. If I couldn't get a loan, how many other people were having their applications rejected? Large-scale demand, at the same time as low supply, was an indication of an ideal environment for business success.

I couldn't figure out how to acquire rental property without cash or a bank loan. It would take a miracle or a change in fortune. In the face of insurmountable odds, I put aside my real estate ambition for the time being and kept working at my three businesses.

# Chapter 8

# Real Estate

Dad called and asked for my help with a property. He had lived there for a while, but had moved away from the area a long time ago. He'd done little maintenance over the years. It was rented out as an artist studio and earned a little as an art gallery. But the income didn't cover the expenses and I thought it was a better idea for him to have extra cash, than to have to keep paying for a property he didn't use.

Since I had more experience with real estate than Dad did, I offered to sell it for him. He said he didn't need the money and asked if I had any investment ideas. I told him about my idea to buy a multi-unit property for rental income. I explained why I didn't have the ability to fund a rental property and suggested that the sale of Dad's place could provide the funds. I'd do all the work and we'd split the profits. Dad liked the idea and he'd been watching my success in real estate, so he felt confident in my ability to put the words into action.

I set out to sell the property. It was in the tiny town of Caspar, a ten minute drive north of Mendocino. I called it Caspar The Friendly Ghost Town. The building was a large hundred-year-old warehouse made of corrugated steel. It had been a bakery and an auto repair garage. Dad turned it into an art gallery. He made a sign that said, "What's A'Foot, a showcase for fine art". He named it without realizing that I'd been involved with Club Foot in San Francisco.

The old-fashioned warehouse was built on a foundation of old-growth redwood, worth more than the entire rest of the structure. From upstairs, there was a peak of ocean view and that alone made it a valuable location. There was no water source, a few times a year a water truck came and filled up a big holding tank in the backyard.

The place had an artsy funky unique personality. Many hundreds of people passed through over the years, enjoying music and art at various events. But it was in bad disrepair. Even though it was insured, I worried somebody might get hurt. Thankfully that never happened. Breezes blew through the building and vines grew through broken windows. Pieces of corrugated steel had blown off the roof and nobody wanted to fix it, because it was too rickety to climb up.

Because of the location and the square footage, many buyers were interested. But because of the condition and lack of water source, no bank would loan on it. Cash buyer bids were too low and the property stayed on the market for many months. Our real estate agent suggested that we offer owner financing.

This was the first time I'd heard of owner financing. The agent reassured me that he'd done a few of these deals before, both for himself and his clients. He explained how it worked. We set the terms and his office provided documents. Everything else stayed the same and closed at a title company as usual.

I called Dad and told him I liked the idea of offering seller financing. It seemed to be a better option than lowering the price or taking it off the market. Dad agreed to try it if the loan was only for five years. The agent modified the listing to include our financing terms. Within a few days, we had several offers. We chose the most qualified buyer and that's how I became a note investor.

After we closed on Dad's property, I was expecting to buy a multi-family rental property. But since we had to carry a note, we only had the down payment to invest. It was a good down payment, but nowhere near enough. My plans had been based on getting a cash sale.

I adjusted my goals to the actual budget restrictions. Instead of buying a multi-family property, I decided to get a condo or mobile home and pay for it in cash. After a couple of years, I could try to qualify for a loan based on the rental income. Eventually, I'd be able to get a small multi-family property.

I couldn't afford anything in the city, but I found an affordable condo an hour away. I offered all the cash I had. My offer was accepted and we went into escrow. A few days later, I had lunch with Mom and told her about the deal. She smiled when I told her Dad was involved, she liked that he was helping me. She thought it was a great idea to have rental property and said she was very proud of me.

But Mom didn't like that I was buying a condo. She had heard me talk about multi-family property before and wanted to know why I changed my plans. She was concerned about Homeowner Association expenses, as well as a lack of independent ownership.

I explained the situation. I told her why I couldn't get a loan because of my self-employment. I filled her in on why the bank wouldn't lend on Dad's property and how we did an installment sale. That was the reason why I only had the down payment to invest. I was making the best of what I had. The condo was what I could afford and I planned to scale up in a couple of years.

While I was confiding in Mom, I mentioned how much I'd lost with the financial advisor. She looked alarmed and asked me to repeat the amount I'd lost. After lunch, when I went back to work, she called the financial advisor and asked about her own funds. She found out she'd lost more than she realized. She called me and asked if I could come over and talk.

Mom was concerned she had everything invested with one financial institution and she wanted to diversify. She had always been interested in real estate, but didn't want the hassle of the work that's involved. She said she'd like to partner with me if I cancelled escrow on the condo and purchased a multi-family building instead. She'd apply for the loan and contribute some of the down payment. I would do all the work.

My parents had been separated for a long time, but they inadvertently came together to invest in my business. I was very grateful and felt blessed that they both believed in me enough to be business partners. I knew it would be profitable for them and not just a favor to me.

I got out of escrow on the condo and started looking for a multi-family property. I found a four-unit apartment building in downtown Santa Rosa. I also found three houses on an acre outside town. I made offers on both properties and both were accepted.

I chose the three houses on an acre. The location was beautiful horse country, in a valley at the foot of a mountain. Bordering the property was a wilderness preserve, protecting natural habitat for native species. The breeze was infused with an intoxicating smell that reminded me of frankincense or myrrh.

I budgeted to improve the property and remodel all three houses. We planned to hold it for long-term cash flow. It was a wonderful plan and a promising property. I was happy and full of optimism for my future. This really was a dream come true.

We were closing escrow on Friday. The title company told us to schedule with a mobile notary on the day of closing. After we signed documents, we were to wire the funds to the title company. We made plans to meet the notary at noon on Friday at Mom's house.

Thursday night Mom didn't feel well and early Friday morning she was rushed to the hospital for emergency surgery. She came through successfully and went to the ICU. I fielded calls from the Title Company, the agents and the notary. Given the circumstances, everyone agreed to delay closing until Monday. That turned out to be overly optimistic and we kept extending the closing. It took a couple of weeks before Mom was well enough to sign papers.

I spent every day with Mom while she was in the hospital and when she got home. In addition to doing everything I could to take care of her, I had to keep up with my other responsibilities. I still had three businesses and now suddenly a multi-unit rental was added to the load. It was a lot of weight to bear, but I put my head down and pushed through.

The rental property was covered in junk and I had it cleaned up. They hauled over a dozen truckloads to the dump and hazard waste site. A new well was drilled and new water pumps were installed. A gardener cut the tall grass and pruned the landscape. Pest control exclusion barriers were put in for all three units. Three new mailboxes were installed, replacing the single one that was rusty and falling over, the mailman stopped to thank me. It was a beautiful property, but had not been cared for and that was why I got a good price on it.

One of the tenants moved out unexpectedly. I took the vacancy as an opportunity to remodel. Even though I was overloaded, and it was before schedule, it made good business sense to remodel before finding new tenants. I went into Bulldozer Effect mode. I hired a crew to update the bathroom, paint the walls, make repairs and haul away junk. I replaced outdated appliances with stainless steel and bought a new water heater. When it was done, I raised the rents.

I was barely handling everything, but the hits just kept on coming. I got home from work and my husband had moved all his possessions out. All I got was a text that said, "Sorry, I couldn't face you". It was just before our fifth anniversary and completely unexpected. I didn't have any warning. I thought we were doing fine and got sucker punched. Breaking up by text was disrespectful and cruel, I was shocked and hurt.

I didn't hear from him again until several months later, when he finally called. He explained he'd been angry with me, mostly because of the real estate business. He was upset when Mom asked him to sign a quitclaim deed. That had been a business decision that her lawyer had insisted on, but he took it personally.

It stunned me that my husband would leave me for doing the very thing that was going to secure our future economically. Maybe that's why he left or maybe not, the whole thing never really made sense to me. He gave some other flimsy reasons, but not one seemed a valid excuse for ending a marriage so suddenly like that.

The way he left with no conversation, just a text message, was heartless. I hadn't done anything wrong and he knew the kind of pressure I'd been under. I accepted that it would ultimately be a good thing he was out of my life. He was not a kind person.

I was unlucky in love. One husband left because I was in the music business. The other left because I was in the real estate business. It would have been funny, if it didn't hurt so much.

Mom was recovering at home and I didn't tell her my husband had left. I didn't want her to be under more stress worrying about me. When she started getting stronger, I finally confided in her and told her my marriage was over. She felt bad for me, but it didn't make her feel worse. She actually seemed to relish the opportunity to focus on my problems, instead of her own.

Mom was doing better every day, until one morning she had a stroke. I rode in the ambulance with her and got to the hospital in time to get treatment. But it was all too much for her and a couple months later, she passed away. All the air was sucked out of the planet and the lights flickered off. I was devastated.

Two days before her passing, I asked Mom if she had any wisdom to share. Her last words of advice to me were like a poem:

Be kind, even when someone doesn't deserve it
Be kind, not because of who they are
But because that's who you are

I'd built my life around three people: my son, my husband and my mom. They were my inner circle, my tribe, my family. Like a three-legged stool that loses two legs, I fell down hard and hit the ground. It was the worst year of my life. I'd been stoic and strong for decades and now I completely fell apart. Every pain I'd ever ignored flooded back, volcanically rising up and scalding me. Negative memories filled my mind and amplified the excruciating loss.

I was consumed by grief. Mom was the one person who always checked for me and made sure I was okay. She was my best friend. My confidant. My music teacher. My supporter. My role model. My heart and soul. Her absence left a Mom-shaped void that nothing else could fill.

I was disoriented and lost, but I still had to keep working. I hired a property manager for the first time. I let them deal with getting new tenants and collecting rent. It took a lot of pressure off me and I was grateful I didn't have to drive an hour in each direction to interview applicants. But management, combined with repairs, swallowed up the profit margin.

I was still in the middle of remodeling one of the houses and couldn't delegate all the decisions. I couldn't afford to stop the work until I felt better and one day I had drive to the property to meet with a contractor. When I got to the property, a tenant came out of his house. He confronted me and started yelling.

He was upset he had to leave at the end of his lease. He'd been given notice seven months before. When I first bought the property, I had notified him I was going to renovate his house and raise the rent at the end of his lease. He and his family could move back in after that, if they wanted to. Now his lease was up in two months and he hadn't found another place yet.

He'd been difficult all along and I'd been making an effort to appease him. His rent was well below market and I didn't increase it. When his laundry machines broke down, I bought new ones, although it wasn't included in the rental agreement. I offered generous cash incentives to leave early. He wasn't appreciative of my efforts. He was always irritable and demanding. His wife was nice and she rolled her eyes in silent solidarity with me.

But she couldn't control her husband, I'm pretty sure he was under the influence of drugs and/or alcohol.

We stood in the yard and he got loud and said mean words. I was in a fragile state and I burst into tears and walked away. I couldn't deal with this bitter tenant who didn't appreciate what it took to provide a home. The rental property had been stressful the whole time, from the original closing day when Mom went to the hospital. In theory, it was a great business opportunity and a dream come true. But in reality, it was unexpectedly difficult and unpleasant.

It didn't seem possible that things could get worse, but then I was forced to sell the rental property. Mom's lawyer had given us bad advice and told us that one partner's ownership could easily become the other's inheritance. But the property got caught up in her estate and I had to sell it. I felt very bad that I lost the rental property, after all the work and heartache. It was the continuation of a relentless drowning feeling, another loss piled on the others. I kept thinking I had hit the bottom, but I was still falling.

Nearly everything I cared about was gone, there wasn't enough left to salvage anything from the past. Life, as I knew it, was erased. I gave up trying to figure out which way was up and what was supposed to be normal and routine. I gave in to the deconstruction. Everything hurt.

My friends asked how I was doing and I was unable to put on my usual brave face. I said I wanted to start from scratch, close my businesses and move away. Everybody strongly warned me not to change anything. They all gave me the same advice: don't make sudden changes while grieving. The general consensus of my friends, and the internet, was to give it a year. I put my faith in their collective wisdom and obediently waited a long depressing year. It was a time of feeling broken and sad. Tears poured down my face every day. I felt dazed and lost.

My son moved from another state to live near me. He must have sensed my despair, although I tried to mask it. He was my only comfort and light in the darkness. His presence reminded me there was something worth living for. Outside the pain, there was a life that was still wonderful and one day things would be better. He put things into perspective, as he always had.

During that year, I didn't know how I went to work or did anything. I was dazed with deep sadness and a sense of being disoriented. I didn't waste the time though. I still had to work and also deal with Mom's belongings.

My thoughts kept circling, evaluating my life and considering what I was going to do next. I had been set on building a portfolio of rental properties, but the bad experience with the tenant changed my mind. It helped to use a property manager as a gatekeeper, but then there wasn't enough profit leftover to make it worth it.

I couldn't help but notice that, compared to being a landlord, owning a note was easier and more profitable. There were no ongoing expenses, no property tax or repairs, no vacancies. The work was negligible once it was set up. The cash flow continued, regardless of where I was or what I was doing. I didn't get phone calls to fix problems. I liked the business model and started learning about the note industry online, in books, taking classes.

After the year was over, I was ready to move forward immediately. I felt like I'd been holding my breath. I took the net from selling the rental property and purchased a home in Sonoma. For many years, I'd been longing to go back to a small town lifestyle. I liked the internal rhyme Nomi from Sonoma, that wasn't the only reason I picked the location, but it tipped the scales.

I had to close down Document Organizer. I found and trained a replacement for each of my clients. I waited the longest to tell Dan Ellsberg. He depended on me and I wanted to wait until a time when it would be the least stressful for him. He had just published his book and was on a national book tour. Steven Spielberg released "The Post" around the same time and Dan was extremely busy.

Once the flurry of the book tour calmed down and they came back from the movie premier, I couldn't delay telling Dan and Patricia my news. I told them I was leaving, but I'd stay with them until after the Oscars, I'd find and train a replacement. It was sad to say goodbye. They were very supportive while I was going through a bad time. I was fond of them and it wasn't easy to tell them I was leaving. It felt like another loss and made me cry. But at the same time, I was glad to stop doing the work.

I knew Document Organizer could have been a bigger company. The demand for my services was much greater than the supply. I could have hired people, written a book, built a brand. That would have put me in a position to sell the business. But instead I gave away my clients to my competitors. I hadn't expanded the business because music occupied my free time. Document Organizer did what I built it to do. It allowed me to make a living, working for myself and setting my own schedule. I felt proud of having built a business that supported my family.

I packed and moved to my new house. I left with a great sense of relief, escaping a place oppressed by sad memories. After I moved to Sonoma, it took me a few months to unwind. I read that the five most stressful events in a person's life were death of a loved one, divorce, moving, job loss and major illness. I had four out of five at the same time, I was thankful for good health.

After I settled into my new home, I sensed that the valley of the shadow of death was retreating and Sonoma Valley was healing me, a little more every day. It was peaceful and beautiful. After all the places I lived, this was the first time I felt at home since leaving Albion.

My son sensed I was doing better and went back to his life, attending school in another state. I had tried acting strong around him and didn't want him to see how much pain I was in. I never asked him to take care of me, but I was very grateful for his kindness. I didn't want him to pause his life for me and was glad when he enrolled in college. I sure did miss him though.

I got a strange feeling inside me that I didn't recognize. It wasn't like being sick, but I felt light and almost dizzy. Then I realized what it was that I was feeling. I was happy. I'd forgotten what happiness felt like.

# Chapter 9

# ELOHE LOANS

I was alone, but the solitude was nourishing. I had no source of income, except occasional royalty checks and interest from one note. I lived on credit cards until I was able to sell my residence in Berkeley. I used the time to continue my education in notes and build my business team and infrastructure.

After a year of educating myself about the note business, there was still more I needed to understand. I worked hard to shorten the learning curve. I traveled to conferences and consulted with experts. The biggest value was in casual conversations with other note investors. They generously shared their knowledge and referrals, so I didn't have to reinvent the wheel. Many went on to become friends and business associates.

I met with top attorneys and CPAs and was disappointed to find that the majority didn't understand the note business. They assured me of their capabilities, but I found that I was explaining terms to them and correcting their misconceptions. One lawyer said he would learn everything he needed to know after I gave him a retainer. He thought I should pay for his education, I thought I was paying for expertise.

There were countless ways to invest in real estate lending and I didn't realize how many different options there were. I ran hundreds of imaginary deals through my calculator to figure out the differences in yields. Returns were impressive, but I had to consider risks. I thought up every potential problem. Each worry led to figuring out how to mitigate the risk. I spent a great deal of time analyzing and visiting locations to invest in, states with good lender laws and strong economies. I learned about local real estate markets and built a team.

As with songwriting and other professions, the note industry appeared easy at first and became more complex the more I knew. Each lesson led to more questions like an unraveling complex problem. I wanted to go faster because I had to earn a living. But I needed to fill the gaps in my knowledge because I couldn't afford mistakes. I thought it would take a few months, but it took another year before I was ready to invest.

I also wanted this business to do more than make money, I wanted it to make a difference in the world. Helping people become homeowners felt like an honorable choice, it felt like right livelihood. Long-term loans created stability and that was good for everyone, borrower and lender. Stability was a consideration, not just maximizing profit.

I made up my mind to focus on seller financing, like my first note. Seller financing was a simple and elegant investment vehicle. Borrowers who couldn't get loans became homeowners. Real estate investors closed more deals. Private lenders made good returns.

It took two years of complication to arrive at simplicity. I approached songwriting the same way, writing and rewriting a dozen pages for a single verse. I often ended up back at the first version, but by then I was confident in my choice. I knew I had tried many options and hadn't settled for the first thing that occurred to me. I was cut from the same cloth as Leonard Cohen, who wrote eighty verses of *Hallelujah* to end up with five.

During this time, I read a book by Mitch Stephen, one of the foremost experts on owner financing, and found that he was also a skilled and prolific songwriter. I had never heard of a songwriter note investor, other than myself. I contacted him and we became friends.

I enrolled in his owner-financing course and learned how sell a house without using a real estate agent. With a high-priced house in Berkeley, this was a significant savings. My friends were concerned and strongly advised me to use an agent. But Mitch had a plan that made sense and I followed his advice instead.

The property was a manufactured house and the banks couldn't find any comparable sales. There were no manufactured houses sold in the past three years in Berkeley. Without comps, it couldn't get through underwriting and the banks wouldn't lend on it. We went in and out of escrow. I advertised that seller financing was available, but it's uncommon in California and people were suspicious.

Finally, I got an offer from a French couple, qualified borrowers who couldn't get a bank loan because they were foreigners. They gave me a big down payment and a promissory note. A few months later, they found a way to refinance and I finally had enough to launch a note business.

I named my business Elohe Loans. I wanted to give a tribute to Dad for helping me get started. Since he read scripture everyday, I thought the Bible was a good place to look for a name. I found the first mention of a real estate transaction in Genesis: "The plot of ground, where he pitched his tent, he purchased for a hundred pieces of silver. There he set up an altar and called it El Elohe Israel" (God is the mighty God of Israel).

After two years of preparation, I finally got the business going. First, I modified the loan on Dad's property. I eliminated the five-year balloon and made it into a fully amortized thirty-year note. This was a big relief to the owner. It took away the stress of the impending balloon and significantly lowered their monthly payment. At the same time, it greatly increased my potential yield.

Next, I made a small commercial automobile loan. The borrower was a professional driver for ridesharing companies. He didn't qualify for credit and was paying an outrageous rate to lease a car. He was very thankful to get a loan that he could afford and it felt good to help him secure his livelihood. I did one other business auto loan, but real estate was better collateral.

I invested in a few deals with an experienced real estate investor, buying seller financed notes he created. This allowed me to see the process first hand. I did some short-term commercial loans with professional lenders to see what documentation and procedures they were using.

For each note I put in my portfolio, I turned down several dozen others. I put each offer under scrutiny and one red flag was all it took to move on to the next. I only made loans to qualified borrowers on houses in good condition in nice neighborhoods. If there was risk of losing principal, I passed on it. When a deal finally got through the filters and under contract, it still had to go to underwriting. I only took slam-dunk deals and considered every worst-case scenario seriously. Life was risky enough without taking on additional challenges.

I frequently heard people mention that they were interested in real estate investing, but didn't have time for it. They asked about the deals I was doing and were impressed at the yields. Their returns from banks were extremely low and Wall Street was unpredictable. Real estate was the most secure way to diversify. I heard some version of this many times.

I didn't need investors and I wasn't thinking of growing the business beyond supporting myself. But when the deal flow exceeded my own funds, I started sharing opportunities. I'd already built an infrastructure and was set up to protect my own portfolio. The heavy lifting was already done and it wouldn't take much to extend the opportunities to other passive lenders.

To add a layer of security, the loans were boarded with a third-party note servicing company, who paid the passive investors directly. The lenders got fixed monthly payments for the term of their notes, even if something happened to me. It was also fascinating to discover the little-known opportunity to use self-directed retirement accounts. A ROTH IRA could invest in notes and make double-digit returns tax-free.

When I started reaching out to friends and neighbors with opportunities to invest, I realized there was a great lack of knowledge.

Even though note investing was lucrative and the risk was mitigated, it was a niche market of real estate investing, relatively unheard of. Educating investors had to be part of my business.

My first passive investors were a couple I'd known for a long time. I wanted to start with a small low-risk loan. They invested $15,000, secured by a note worth $30,000, on a property worth $65,000. The interest rate was 8% and they would collect a monthly payment of $182 for ten years. If the loan went to the end of the term, their total profit would be $6,839 with a 45.59% return.

Every time a passive investor invested in a note, it allowed me the ability to offer someone an opportunity to become a homeowner. This was meaningful to me beyond being a way to make a living. The business had the higher purpose of helping families and having a positive impact on neighborhoods.

# Chapter 10

# ON NOTES TO NOTES

I'm in awe of the power of music. Songwriting has a profound effect on me, it's my therapy and my expression. I'm grateful for the encouragement my listeners have given me. It's a gift when someone is moved by one of my songs. I deeply appreciate how fortunate I am to have followed music as a career.

When I was a child, I was an artist and music was my pure passion. When I became a professional musician, I had to become an entertainer. I had chosen a profession as a songwriter and it was an unpleasant shock to find out that I had apparently selected the entertainment industry. What was spiritual became commercial, what was precious became a coomodity.

Music is not the music industry. The first time I really understood that was on a Saturday night, playing a packed club in downtown San Jose. From the stage, I looked over to the side of the room. Audience members were thickly crowded at the bar. Four bartenders were busy pouring drinks and taking money.

I looked to the back of the room, by the door. The promoter was on a stool behind a podium. He was selling tickets and putting the money in a cash drawer. His eyes kept glancing over to the band playing onstage. He was smiling and nodding in time to the music.

I was wearing a miniskirt and high heels. I danced the entire show, bouncing my hands on the keyboards, smiling and looking cool. This was a big city weekend in a nightclub with a hot reggae dancehall lineup and I was the girl in the band. I put out a lot of energy and embraced being an entertainer, it paid the bills.

I was good at projecting a party vibe, but that night it was fake. It was a *Tears Of A Clown* situation. On the outside, I was partying in a club on a Saturday night. On the inside, I was having a sinking revelation about the music business. What I realized that night is that music is not an industry for artists. The music business is a loss leader for the alcohol industry.

I had learned about loss leaders, it's the toy inside a box of cereal. If a kid wants the toy, they have to buy the cereal. The product is the cereal and the loss leader is the toy. People come to concerts to hear music, but the real product is alcohol and the loss leader is music. Musicians are there to sell alcohol. That's when I stopped thinking that being a musician made me important.

I kept on performing anyway, that night in San Jose and for hundreds more shows to come. It was something I was good at and it was easy to get gigs. But I didn't love it. I never meant to be an alcohol salesman or an entertainer. I'm a songwriter. But I'm grateful for my career as a performer, it made for an interesting job.

Being in the music industry is like living in a funny mirror. Musicians are given a reverence beyond their actual usefulness. I recognize the importance of music, but I don't think musicians deserve that kind of idolization. The music business is not as vital as it pretends to be. Music nourishes us, but it isn't food, shelter or health. Comparatively, it isn't that important.

I had a conversation about music with Mom. I confided my worry that I'd spent my life pursuing something that wasn't worthwhile. She was surprised when I burst into tears. Mom suggested I consider the message in the songs I was writing. She said I could infuse meaning into the writing. I took her advice to heart and from that time on I write songs with intention.

Conscious songwriting is wonderful, but people are struggling to survive and I want to contribute something more tangible than art. The note business provides me with a meaningful way of giving back to society. Music is nourishing to the spirit, while real estate is tangible. A song is a three-minute series of sound waves in the air that mystically touch the soul. But a house is shelter, a primary human need.

Originally, I became a note investor because it seemed like a good business and it is good. I can work from home and set my own hours. I can achieve my economic goals, to have an income and prepare for later in life.

But, in addition to being a good livelihood, I've been unexpectedly gratified to discover that the note business has the capacity to make things better for others. It helps a number of different people during the course of ordinary business.

#1 The Borrower: The note business helps people become homeowners. The borrowers are sincere and hardworking. They're blocked from bank credit for being self-employed or a variety of other reasons. They are grateful for the opportunity and determined to hold onto their homes. Going from a renter to a homeowner can alter the course of their lives, for their family and future generations. I like not being a landlord, there's only one Lord and it isn't me. I like providing an alternative to banks. Elohe Loans is part of building an independent economy and facilitating the American Dream.

#2 The Entrepreneur: The note business helps real estate investors make a better living, because they are able to offer seller financing to their buyers. Those real estate investors hire local construction companies and services. They improve the neighborhoods they invest in.

#3 The Seller: The note business helps sellers get their properties sold. Many homes and buyers can't qualify for traditional financing, for any number of reasons. Private lending solves problems with creative deal structures. It stimulates the housing market and improves property values.

#4 The Lender: The note business helps passive investors earn better returns. They don't have to fight to stay ahead of inflation. They can get good yields and diversify from banks and Wall Street. The passive investor is given an opportunity to receive a fixed monthly income and invest in real estate, without having to own property.

For retiring seniors, Elohe Loans creates cash flow, with above average yields, while helping families become homeowners. It's a win-win-win-win situation and a rewarding business model. I'm honored to have landed in the position where I can participate in something that is beneficial for everyone involved. It has the most impact of my countless occupations.

Elohe Loans was made possible by my first note. That's when I learned the concept of seller financing and got seed money for real estate. From the beginning, Dad said it could be a family-owned business. That came true between him and I right away, later Mom joined in. It came full circle when my son started partnering with me, providing invaluable skills in sales and marketing. Elohe Loans is truly a family-owned business, as Dad's vision was manifested in unexpected ways.

    I never would have guessed that the music business would lead to the note business. It felt like a twisting road of random chaos. But maybe it wasn't chance. Maybe it was mystical alignment.

    I had my share of love and loss, low and high, same as anyone. I met famous people and stumbled into history like Forrest Gump. I moved a lot and didn't feel like I belonged anywhere. Poverty, and fear of poverty, drove me to being an entrepreneur. The Bulldozer Effect taught me how to use strength of will to conquer obstacles. I chased and caught dreams.

    I was in sketchy situations over and over, but I don't blame the world. I've come to realize that being repeatedly exposed to danger is a symptom, like recurring nightmares. Lucid dreaming controls the nightmares and I rarely have them anymore. Lucid living replaces stress and danger with calm and joy.

    I continue to work as a songwriter and artist coach. I got my wish to return to being an artist, after a life as an entertainer. I'm grateful for the interesting experiences in my past and optimistic about the future.

Here in the present, I'm at peace. I write and play music every day. My recording studio is graced by Mom's baby grand piano. Elohe Loans is a growing business that I enjoy. I'm in love with my beautiful town and finally feel at home. I maintain good health, exercising and drinking water.

Music and real estate, both add value and meaning to my life. I'm blessed from notes to notes.

A GIG IN NASHVILLE

A LIMO IN SAN DIEGO

A PROMO PICTURE

EEK-A-MOUSE

# Appendix 1

# Examples

## Disclaimer

Examples are provided for educational purposes only. The examples are descriptions of actual notes in my portfolio. The numbers have been rounded for the sake of simplification and some notes may have changed since publication. These examples are intended to illustrate my business model and are not intended to be advertisements or professional advice. Contact the publisher to learn about investing in current notes.

Nomi Yah Music
NomiYahMusic@gmail.com
707-931-1396
19050 Bay Street #42, El Verano, CA 95433

# EXAMPLE 1

The owner lived in this Texas house and remodeled much of it over the years. She moved for health reasons and put the home on the market. A real estate investor purchased it with a note from Elohe Loans. It will be sold with seller financing to a qualified buyer. This will create a long-term note and an investment opportunity for a passive lender.

| | |
|---|---|
| Note to Owner | $150,000 |
| Term | 30 Years |
| Monthly Payment | $1,261 |
| Note from Passive Investor | $62,200 |
| Term | 5 Years |
| Interest Rate | 8.00% |
| Monthly Payment | $1,261 |
| **Passive Investor Yield** | **21.67%** |

# EXAMPLE 2

This property didn't qualify for a bank loan. A buyer purchased it with seller financing for her daughter, who lives there and operates a craft store. The original note had a five-year balloon. Elohe Loans modified it to thirty years and lowered the monthly payment. The borrowers were happy and the loan was more stable.

| | |
|---|---|
| Note to Owner | $138,000 |
| Term | 5 Years |
| Monthly Payment | $1,160 |
| Modified Note | $115,000 |
| Term | 30 Years |
| Monthly Payment | $823 |
| Note from Passive Investor | $41,600 |
| Term | 5 Years |
| Interest Rate | 7.00% |
| Monthly Payment | $823 |
| **Passive Investor Yield** | **18.83%** |

# EXAMPLE 3

The owner is a real estate investor who purchased this off-market Texas house with a hard money loan. Elohe Loans paid off the balloon with a new first lien. The 30% Loan To Value ratio makes this one of the most secure loans in the portfolio. The buyer is a construction worker and has improved the value of the house significantly.

| | |
|---|---|
| Note to Owner | $22,500 |
| Term | 15 Years |
| Monthly Payment | $241 |
| | |
| Note from Passive Investor | $11,900 |
| Term | 5 Years |
| Interest Rate | 8.08% |
| Monthly Payment | $241 |
| **Passive Investor Yield** | **21.91%** |

# EXAMPLE 4

A real estate investor found this Texas house for a low price because it was in receivership. Elohe Loans provided the funds for the purchase. The owner is repairing the house and selling it with seller financing. When he finds a qualified buyer, the note will be transferred to the new owner. This will create an investment opportunity for a passive lender.

| | |
|---|---|
| Note to Owner | $185,000 |
| Term | 30 Years |
| Monthly Payment | $1,555 |
| Note from Passive Investor | $76,700 |
| Term | 5 Years |
| Interest Rate | 8.01% |
| Monthly Payment | $1,555 |
| **Passive Investor Yield** | **21.69%** |

# EXAMPLE 5

This Texas house was purchased with a short-term hard money loan by a real estate investor. Elohe Loans paid off the balloon with a new first lien. The owner sold the property with seller financing to a contractor, who didn't qualify for a bank loan because he was self-employed. He has put in significant labor and material, greatly improving the value of the house. He's a hard-working entrepreneur who deserves to become a homeowner.

| | |
|---|---|
| Note to Owner | $27,000 |
| Term | 15 Years |
| Monthly Payment | $290 |
| Note from Passive Investor | $14,300 |
| Term | 5 Years |
| Interest Rate | 8.02% |
| Payment | $290 |
| **Passive Investor Yield** | **21.73%** |

# EXAMPLE 6

This Texas property is five acres zoned for urban residential lots. The owner is a real estate developer who purchased the property with cash. He plans to build twenty houses on the property. Elohe Loans gave him a first lien note so he could pay delinquent property taxes and development costs. After five months, he qualified for commercial bank funding and paid off the loan.

| | |
|---|---|
| Note to Owner | $75,000 |
| Term | 1 Year |
| Monthly Payment | $687 |
| **Yield** | **11%** |

# Example 7

This Texas property is a house with seven acres. The neighborhood has thousands of new houses in construction. The owner is a real estate developer who plans to build storage units on the property and use the house for an onsite manager's family. He expects to get a commercial loan with a lower interest rate in the near future and pay off the note from Elohe Loans.

| | |
|---|---|
| Note to Owner | $300,000 |
| Term | 3 Years |
| Monthly Payment | $2,000 |
| **Yield** | **8.00%** |

# EXAMPLE 8

This is a house in Texas on fifteen acres with a barn. A real estate investor purchased it off-market with funds from Elohe Loans. He's repairing the house and selling it. If he finds a buyer qualified for seller financing, the note can be transferred to the new owner. This would create an investment opportunity for a passive lender.

| | |
|---|---|
| Note to Owner | $75,000 |
| Term | 30 Years |
| Monthly Payment | $658 |
| Note from Passive Investor | $32,400 |
| Term | 5 Years |
| Interest Rate | 8.07% |
| Monthly Payment | $658 |
| **Passive Investor Yield** | **21.88%** |

# EXAMPLE 9

This property was difficult to finance because it is a manufactured house. The banks couldn't find comparable sales in the area because the town didn't have manufactured homes. Elohe Loans offered seller financing to a qualified couple. In three months, they found a lender with better terms and refinanced.

| | |
|---|---|
| First Lien | $650,000 |
| Term | 30 Years |
| Monthly Payment | $3,897 |
| **Yield** | **7.19%** |

# EXAMPLE 10

The owner is a real estate investor who purchased this off-market home using a short-term hard money loan with a balloon. He borrowed from Elohe Loans to pay off the balloon with a new first lien. Four months later, the owner sold the property and paid the loan in full.

| | |
|---|---|
| Note to Owner | $29,500 |
| Term | 15 Years |
| Monthly Payment | $317 |
| **Yield** | **9.95%** |

# Appendix 2

# BIBLIOGRAPHY

Alan Cowgill
- *How To Get All The Money You Need To Buy Property*

Anne Marie Hamilton
- *Living In Shashamane*

Art Boericke and Barry Shapiro
- *Handmade Houses: A Guide to the Woodbutcher's Art*

Aryae Coopersmith
- *Holy Beggars: A Journey From Haight Street To Jerusalem*

Baba Ram Dass
- *Be Here Now*

Bob Zachmeier
- *Who Needs The Bank? Why You Should Be A Bank Instead Of Investing In One*
- *Upside Up: Successful Strategies To Make Money In Any Market*

Brian Davison
- *The Top Ten Pitfalls Of Trust Deed And Mortgage Investing: Personal Investor Risk Management In Hard Money, Private Lending And Real Estate Notes*

Cameron Lancaster
- *The Passive Income Playbook: How Real Estate And Private Investment Can Help You Get Rich And Retire Early*

Chelsea Cain
- *Wild Child: Girlhoods In The Counterculture*

Colby Buzzell
- *My War: Killing Time In Iraq*

Daniel Ellsberg
- *Doomsday Machine: Confessions Of A Nuclear War Planner*
- *Secrets: A Memoir Of Vietnam And The Pentagon Papers*

Dave Dictor
- *MDC: Memoir From A Damaged Civilization*

Dave Knudson
- *The Art Of The Loan*

Dave Van Horn
- *Introduction To Note Investing*
- *Real Estate Note Investing: Using Mortgage Notes To Passively And Massively Increase Your Income*

Dawn Rickabaugh
- *Seller Financing On Steroids: Pumping Paper For Power, Peace And Profits*

Don Loyd
- *An Insider's Guide To Private Lending: How To Safely Earn 10% To 20% Returns On Your Money Without Being A Landlord Or Flipping Houses*

Eddie Speed
- *Streetwise Seller Financing*

Eek-A-Mouse
- *WaDoDem*

Evvy Eisen
- *Multiply By Six Million: Portraits And Stories Of Holocaust Survivors*

George Anton
- *The Banker's Code*
- *The Debt Millionaire: Most People Will Never Build Real Wealth. Now You Can Be One Of The Few Who Do*

Grandmaster Flash, Edward G. Fletcher, Melle Mel, Sylvia Robinson, Clifton Chase

- *The Message*

Gustavo Gomez
- *Private Money Lending: Learn How To Consistently Generate A Passive Income Stream*

Jack Bosch
- *Forever Cash: Break The Earn Spend Cycle, Take Charge Of Your Life, Build Everlasting Wealth*

Jason Mulgrew
- *Everything Is Wrong With Me: A Memoir Of An American Childhood Gone, Well, Wrong*

Jimmy Napier
- *Invest In Debt: The How To Book On Buying Paper For Cash Flow*

Joanna Rose
- *Little Miss Strange*

Karl Linn
- *Building Commons And Community*

Lee J. Carney
- *Private Lending Profits: Earn 10% To 20% Return On Investment Without Dealing With Tenants*

Lisa Michaels
- *Split: A Counterculture Childhood*

Lorelei Stevens
- *Fast Cash: How I Made A Fortune Buying Notes*

Mark Podolsky
- *Dirt Rich: How One Ambitiously Lazy Geek Created Passive Income In Real Estate Without Renters, Renovations And Rehabs*
- *Passive Income Blueprint*

Sarah Josepha Hale
- *Mary Had A Little Lamb*

Mat Sorenson
- *The Self-Directed IRA Handbook: An Authoritative Guide To Self-Directed Retirement Plan Investors And Their Advisors*

Maxine Swann
- *Flower Children*

Michael Ellsberg
- *Nicole Milner Tribute*
- *The Last Safe Investment: Spending Now To Increase Your True Wealth Forever*
- *The Education Of Millionaires: It's Not What You Think And It's Not Too Late*
- *The Power Of Eye Contact: Your Secret For Success In Business, Love And Life*
- *Funny A\*\* Stories*

Micah Perks
- *Pagan Time: An American Childhood*

Michelle Obama
- *Becoming*

Mitch Stephen

- *My Life & 1000 Houses: The Art Of Owner Financing*
- *My Life & 1000 Houses: Failing Forward To Financial Freedom*
- *My Life & 1000 Houses: 200+ Ways To Find Bargain Properties*

Napoleon Hill
- *Think And Grow Rich*

Norman Mailer
- *Marilyn: The Untold Story*

Renee Lertzman
- *Interview with Karl Linn, Ecopsychologist and Entrepreneur*

River
- *Dwelling: On Making Your Own*

Robert Allen
- *Nothing Down: Dynamic New Wealth Strategies In Real Estate*

Rodney Miller
- *Private Lending: How To Make Double-Digit Returns Lending Money To Real Estate Investors*

Ron LeGrand
- *The Less I Do, The More I Make: How To Get More Done In Less Time And Take Your Life Back*

Sandra Eugster

- *Notes From Nethers: Growing Up In A Commune*

Sarah Josepha Hale
- *Mary Had A Little Lamb*

Simon Sinek
- *Start With Why: How Great Leaders Inspire Everyone To Take Action*

Smokey Robinson, Stevie Wonder, Hank Cosby
- *Tears Of A Clown*

Tom Henderson
- *Note Professor Notebook: Your Key To Unlock The Doors To Knowledge, Profit, Wealth*

Tommy Newberry
- *Success Is Not An Accident: Change Your Choices; Change Your Life*

Wikipedia
- *Burning Man*
- *Karl Linn*
- *Jello Biafra*
- *Henry Rollins*

Willow Yamauchi
- *Adult Child Of Hippies*

# PODCASTS

Bigger Pockets
Broads In Business
Capital Markets Today
Carrot Cast
Forever Cash Life
Investor Army
NNG Note Academy
Note Buying Cash Machine
Note Inc
Note MBA
Owner Financing & Note Investing
Passion For Real Estate
Real Estate Investor Summit
Slate's Negotiation Army
TED Talks Business
The Auto Finance Roadmap
The Best Passive Income Model
The Fearless Pursuit Of Freedom
The Land Geek
The Mentor Podcast
The Private Lender Podcast
Think Realty

# Appendix 3

# Nomi Yah Biography

**Nomi Yah** is a Songwriter. She co-wrote the song *King Of Kings*, currently with Capitol. It was recorded by the band Petra on their gold album P*etra Praise: The Rock Cries Out*, top ten on the charts for a year, winner of a Dove Award. She signed her first publishing deal when she was a teenager with Maranatha Music. She co-wrote *Prison* with Eek-A-Mouse on *Eeksperience* album. She managed the West Coast Songwriters Berkeley Chapter at the Freight & Salvage for fourteen years, co-managed their annual conference, and founded an annual lyric contest.

Nomi has been signed or affiliated with numerous publishers including Maranatha Music, Word, Universal, Capitol, EMI, Brentwood-Benson, Gospel Music Coalition, Corinthian Group, The Copyright Company, CCLI. She won awards including the ASCAP Plus Popular Music Award five times, Tonos A&R Pick, Sherrill C. Corwin Metropolitan Theaters Writing Award, Creative Arts Academic Award.

Her songs have been on Comcast cable commercials, MTV reality shows, the Sundance channel and independent films, including *Champion Bubbla*, *Jammin For Jamaica*, *Island Paradise*. Her music has aired on radio stations including KPFA, KALX, KMFB, Cabo Mil Radio. She was an extra in the movie *Marilyn: The Untold Story*.

Nomi performed for twenty-five years and played over a thousand shows with a wide range of artists from Eek A Mouse to The Flying Karamazov Brothers. She toured throughout the US and internationally. She has been a promoter for clubs and festivals, including Ashkenaz, Freight & Salvage, Palookaville.

She published a book of her original songs, the Nomi Yah Songbook. She published the magazine *Revolutionary Wanker*. She edited *Living In Shashamane* by Anne Marie Hamilton. She wrote the memoir *Notes To Notes: How I Went From Music To Real Estate*.

## SOME ARTISTS NOMI WORKED WITH:

Adam Nielson, Ahkil Mustafa, Ameir Smith, Amlak Tafari, Ana Coates, Andrew Adair Milne, Ann Rosencranz, Area Leader Music Syndicate, Ashling Cole, Azeem, Beth Custer, Brimstone, Cannon and the Lion of Judah, Caribbean Vibe, Cheb I Sabbah, Chika Shimojima, Claytoven, Clocks, C Major Group, Contraband, Culture Kanute, CSBV, Danilo, Dark Circus, Dave Maurichat, Denis Louiseau, Dennis D' Menace, Dr. Jinglez, Dread and the Chosen Few, Eek-A-Mouse, Elio Schiavo, Emsley Fraser and Razor Blade, Faisel, Found Objects, Foundation, Genie Majeeda, George and the Wonders, Glorianna Opera Company, Grand Son Demus, Gulf Of The Farralones, Hurricane Gilbert, Invertebrates, Itals, James Gardiner, Jules Beckman (Blue Man Group), Jeff "4-way" Miller (Bad Posture), Jeff Mooney,

Jess Curtis, John Mazzei, Josh Friedman, Junior B, Keith Hennessy, Karamazov Brothers and the Fighting Instruments Of Karma, Kristyle, Kulture Kanute, Kwama Roots Mama , Lady Saw, Lennon Leppert, Lennox Brown aka Buppy and the Uplifters, Lickshot, Lionel Randolph, Lisa Abraham, Lisa Mischke, Living Theater, Locura De Amor, Love Goat, Lucky Kat, Majah P, Majestic, Major Terror, Malaika Wanag, Marcus Barone, Mark Eitzel and the American Music Club, Melbourne, Mike Lounibos, Moon Has Fat Thighs, Nao Bustamante, Nina Wise, Obeyjah, Oonka Symeon, Phil Nudelman, Quinn Martin, Ralph Eno and the Twitchers, Ralph Kinsey aka Kinsey Report, Rachel Kaplan, Rankin Joe, Ras D, Raskidus, Ras Midas, Red I, Richard Marriott and Club Foot Orchestra, Ron "Hookstown" Brown, Rusty Water Dream Band, Ryan Daisley, Sarah Shelton Mann, Sharon Matthews, Sister I Live, Sly Fox, Sonar Eclipse, Song Brigade, Stanya Kahn, Starhawk and the Black Cat Band, Stevie Love, Sweet Chocolate, Tequila, The Backups, Theater of Changes, Theater Action Group (TAG), Thousand Days Of Shame, Tribal Warning, Toho, Tony D, Traumschuhe, Trinity Rayne, Triplex, Twelve Year Olds, Twisted Roots,

Unda P, Vince Black, Wadi Gad, XSample, YahWanag, Yellow Wall Dub, Zoe & Molly Flores (Starflightrocks), Sweet Chocolate.

## SOME ARTISTS NOMI SHARED THE BILL WITH:

Abyssinians, Alpha Blondy, Andrew Tosh, Anthony B, Arkansas Man, Barry Valentino, Bedlam Rovers, Ben Bacot, Born Jamericans, Buju Banton, Chris Isaak, Clan Dyken, Dominique Baraka, Donny Rasta and Roots Vibration, Elbows Akimbo, Frankie Paul, Fully Fullwood Band, Grandson Demus, Higher Heights, Invertebrates, Israel Vibrations, Itals, J. Scott, Jah Levi, Junior Toots, King Caleb, Kingston 12, Kosono, KuKuKu, Leon Caldero, Lucky Dube, Luciano, Makka B, Mad Professor, Michael Franti, Michael Rose, Mighty Diamonds, Mimimal Man, Pato Banton, Rankin Scroo and Ginger, Reggae Angels, Sanchez, Scropes, Sean Paul, Skatalites, Sly and Robbie, Stacy Golden, Steve Seskin, Taco Wagon, The Dave, Trini-Kid, Vibes Supreme, Wailers, Yami Bolo, Zodiac Sound.

## SOME VENUES WHERE NOMI PERFORMED:
## CALIFORNIA

<u>Alameda</u> - Island Paradise
<u>Belmont</u> - Chris' New Harbor
<u>Berkeley</u> - Ashkenaz, Club Chibbo, Freight & Salvage, Juneteenth Festival, Seen Festival at People's Park, University of California Berkeley
<u>Boulder Creek</u> - Boulder Creek Brewery
<u>Chico</u> - Chico State University
<u>Concord</u> – Brian Wilson Vigil
<u>Davis</u> - University of California Davis
<u>Fresno</u> – Club Fred
<u>Isla Vista</u>- Borsodi's
<u>La Honda</u> – Greenpeace Benefit
<u>Los Angeles</u> – Key Club, Kulak's Woodshed, Roxy Theater, The Gig, Universal Studio City
<u>Mendocino</u> – Greenwood Theater Company, Glorianna Opera Company, Helen Schoeni Theater at the Mendocino Art Center, Mendocino High School, Preston Hall
<u>Monterey</u> - Monterey Bay Reggae Festival
<u>Mount Shasta</u> – Mount Shasta World Music Festival
<u>Oakland</u> - Club Jjang Ga, Continental Club, FM Smith Recreation Center, Reggae in the Hills, Sweet Jimmy's, Uptown Nightclub
<u>Palo Alto</u> - Fanny & Alexander's

Pamona – Glass House
Petaluma – Pheonix Theater
Sacramento - Jamaica House, Red Lion Inn, Ricki's, Scratch 8, Annual Harvest Festival, Ocean Lounge, Stoney Inn, Club Element, OK Universe Sports Complex, Cheers Lounge, RoadHouse
San Diego - Belly Up Tavern, House Of Blues, Viejas Casino, Wave House
Santa Ana - Galaxy
San Francisco – 509 Club, Bamboo Hut, Blue House, Club Foot, Compound, Eagles Tavern, El Rio, Fort Mason, Great American Music Hall, Haight Street Fair, Jelly's, Jillian's At The Metreon, Juneteenth Festival on Fillmore, Klub Komotion, Mabuhay Gardens, Maritime Hall, New College, On Broadway, Paradise Lounge, Pier 23, Rad Cult Fest, Reggae in Golden Gate Park, Shotwell Rogue Loft, Slim's, Sound of Music, Storyville, Valencia Tool and Die, San Francisco Women's Building, Suburban Palace, The Blue House, Full Moon Saloon, Pier 50, New College, I-Hotel, ATA Gallery, Julian Theater, Studio #4, 509 Cultural Center
San Jose – Waves, Agenda Lounge, Club Ibex, Fuel, Cesar Chavez Plaza
San Juan Capistrano - The Coach House
San Leandro - Kicks

San Rafael – Fourth Street Tavern
Santa Barbara - The Coach House, The Shack
Santa Cruz - University of California Santa Cruz, Positively Front Street, Vet's Hall, Catalyst, Palookaville, Brookdale Lodge, San Lorenzo Park, AIDS Walk, Greenpeace Music Festival, Santa Cruz Farmer's Market, Louden Nelson Center, Pacific Cultural Center
Santa Rosa – Sonoma County Fair
Sonoma – The Moose
**COLORADO**
Boulder - Tulagi
**ENGLAND**
Canterbury - ?
London – ?
**GERMANY**
Berlin – Theaterfestival Berliner in Ballhaus Tiergarten, Hochschule de Kunst, Neue HDK,
**HOLLAND**
Amsterdam – ?
**MARYLAND**
Baltimore - 8X10 Room
**MASSACHUSETTES**
Cambridge - House of Blues
Nantucket - The Muse
Northampton - Pearl Street
Oaks Bluff – The Lamp Post
**MEXICO**

Cabo San Lucas – Cabo Wabo, Cabo Mil Festival
**MICHIGAN**
Royal Oak - Fifth Avenue Billiards
**NEW YORK**
New York City - Joe's Pub at the Public Theater, Brooklyn Believer's Church, Brooklyn College
Buffalo – Calumet
**NORTH CAROLINA**
Kill Devil Hills - Port-O-Call
Wilmington - Saxons By The River
**OHIO**
Cleveland - Agora Theater
**OREGON**
Eugene – The Wild Duck, Oregon Country Fair, Wow Hall
Portland – Berbati's Pan, Roseland Theater
**RHODE ISLAND**
Matunuck - Ocean Mist
**SOUTH CAROLINA**
Charleston - The Music Farm
**SPAIN**
Cadeques – Los Pirates.
Barcelona - ?
Empuriabrava – Malibu Club
Gerona - ?
Rosas - ?

**TENNESSEE**
Nashville - Nashville Songwriter's Festival on Music Row, Curb Records, American Songwriter Magazine, Sure Fire Music
**UTAH**
Salt Lake City - Safari Club
**VIRGINIA**
Hampton - Mill Point Park
**WASHINGTON**
Seattle – Bohemian Club, Doc Maynards

# Appendix 4

# Nicole Milner Biography

**Nicole Milner** (March 13, 1937 – February 16, 2017) was a composer, songwriter and pianist. Throughout her life, she performed her original compositions on piano with a unique approach to improvisation. No two performances were alike.

She wrote *It's A Joy To Get To Know You* recorded by Shaina Noll. Her music is on the soundtrack of the documentary *Multiply By Six Million*, nominated for an Emmy. She recorded solo albums *North Coast* and *Free Association*.

She composed and performed for theater, dance and film, and recorded albums with several groups. Her music is regularly played in healing environments, used by massage therapists, physical therapists, spas, recovery rooms, and meditation classes.

Born in Brussels, Nicole and her family fled Belgium in 1940, after the German invasion, and settled in New York City. Milner began studying piano at age seven. Later she attended the High School of Music and Art. She graduated from Barnard in 1956 with a degree in Sociology.

After marrying and having three children, she moved with her family, eventually settling in Albion, on the Mendocino coast of California. She joined a lively arts and music scene that was flourishing in the area.

An involved and important part of the community, Nicole helped found the Headlands School, an alternative private school in Mendocino. She spearheaded the Albion Community Center, which included an early health food coop, one of the first in the nation. She entered a UNICEF-sponsored international children's music contest for Year of the Child in 1979. Her song *Peaceful World* won for the United States.

In 1980, she moved to the Bay Area and finished her degree in Masters of Social Work at San Francisco State University. In 1992, she married Karl Linn, a prominent landscape architect. Linn had worked on the Seagram's Building and Four Seasons restaurant in New York City. He was a pioneer of urban community gardens.

In addition to being a composer and pianist, Nicole was an activist and a longtime pillar of the community. She brought people together, hosting hundreds of meetings in her home. She was actively involved with KPFA, community gardens, Holocaust survivors groups, and various music groups. The city of Berkeley declared a day in her honor.

Reflecting on her life, she wrote, "Over and over I have been amazed at how hard, even horrendous, events in my life, have led to later experiences which have made my life so much richer than before. There is much mystery here…. My experiences have made me acutely aware of the fragility and preciousness of life…. I've been given many blessings and am very grateful for the immense gift of this life."

# Appendix 5

# Karl Linn Biography

**Karl Linn** (March 11, 1923 – February 3, 2005) was a landscape architect, psychologist, educator, and community activist. He was best known for inspiring and guiding the creation of neighborhood commons on vacant lots in East Coast inner cities, during the 1960s through 1980s. Employing a strategy he called "urban barn raising," he engaged neighborhood residents and volunteers in designing and constructing gathering spaces in neighborhoods. In the 1990s, his focus shifted to creating commons in community gardens. Academic colleagues and architectural experts consider Linn to be the father of American Participatory Architecture.

Linn grew up on a fruit tree farm in Dessow, a small village nearly sixty miles northwest of Berlin. His mother had purchased twelve acres in 1913. She designed and supervised the building of a house, planted orchards, and named the property the "Immenhof" (bee house). The farm was an accredited training center for gardeners.

In 1921, his mother married Josef Linn, a widower. Josef was Chief Librarian of the Jewish Community Center in Berlin. He had edited *Hakeshet* (The Rainbow), the first magazine of Modern Hebrew writers and poets, published from 1903 to 1906. He wrote a seminal reference book on the evolution of the Hebrew press, first published in 1928.

The only Jews in their village, the Linns became a target for Nazi persecution. They were forced to flee to Palestine in 1934. The Linn family started a small farm near Haifa, and, at age fourteen, Karl left school to farm and support his parents, who had become too sick to work. He returned to school and graduated from an agricultural high school and helped found a kibbutz. In Tel Aviv, he directed an elementary school gardening program that engaged students in growing food for their own lunches.

Karl entered psychoanalysis, driven to understand the prejudice, brutality, and fanaticism he had experienced. At age twenty-three, he moved to Switzerland and was trained as a psychoanalyst at the Institute for Applied Psychology in Zurich. He immigrated to New York in 1948 and decided to re-enter landscape architecture, which he felt had potential as a healing profession.

Starting as a laborer, Karl gradually developed a landscape contracting business and later a highly respected private practice in landscape architecture. His most prestigious project was designing an interior landscape for The Four Seasons Restaurant in the newly constructed Seagram Building in New York. His groundbreaking work helped pave the way for the emerging field of large-scale interior landscape architecture.

He designed landscapes for affluent owners of residential and corporate properties in and around Manhattan and along the Eastern seaboard. Despite critical acclaim and the satisfaction of designing beautiful spaces, he was increasingly disturbed by the social isolation his designs reinforced and disheartened by the declining social relevance of his work.

In 1959, he accepted an invitation to join the Landscape Architecture department at the University of Pennsylvania in Philadelphia as a full-time faculty member. Karl's innovative curriculum for first-year graduate students engaged them as artists and philosophers, as crafts persons and social activists. Karl took his students into inner city neighborhoods, where they provided community design-and-build services to the economically-disenfranchised residents. Using a participatory process, they engaged residents with volunteer work teams in designing and constructing neighborhood commons, community gathering places on derelict vacant lots. Karl likened this "urban barn raising" to his experience as a young man in Palestine, collaboratively building a kibbutz.

While at Penn, Karl developed a strong friendship with architect Louis Kahn, a fellow professor. When the dean argued that Karl was confusing landscape architecture with social service, Kahn wrote him a letter explaining the value of Karl's approach to the students' development.

Karl pioneered community design-and-build centers, which became models for the Domestic Peace Corp, the Neighborhood Renewal Corps of Philadelphia and the Neighborhood Commons of Washington, D.C. He developed a landscape technicians training program for high school dropouts in Washington, D.C. and then expanded that program into eight other cities. For twenty-five years Linn served on the faculties of MIT and New Jersey Institute of Technology. He gave lectures and workshops at conferences and universities throughout the world. He was an activist for nuclear disarmament and co-founded the Architects, Designers And Planners For Social Responsibility.

Linn moved to the Bay Area, where he co-founded the Urban Habitat Program. Their mission was to develop multicultural environmental leadership and restore inner-city neighborhoods. Linn served on the board of the San Francisco League of Urban Gardeners, the board of Berkeley Partners for Parks and the steering committee of Berkeley's Community Gardening Collaborative. He co-founded East Bay Urban Gardeners and the People of Color Greening Network. Linn often spoke and wrote about the need to reclaim the commons and counter the ongoing privatization of public lands. He believed that guidelines to secure public land for community gardens should be incorporated in cities' general plans. He was convinced that through the creation of community garden commons, neighborhoods would become arenas for extended family living.

In 1993, for his seventieth birthday, a community garden in north Berkeley was dedicated in his name, to honor his lifelong service to community and peace. During the next two years Linn worked with neighbors, volunteers, landscape architecture students, and AmeriCorps teams to revitalize the garden and add a handcrafted seating area and water fountain.

With an overflowing wait list for plots in the refurbished Karl Linn Community Garden, he set his sights on a large weed-filled vacant lot across the street, where the light rail tracks of the Bay Area Rapid Transit (BART) entered an underground tunnel. In 1995, he and City Council representative Linda Maio began to negotiate with BART for use of the land. Karl proceeded to coordinate the planning and construction of the Peralta and Northside Community Gardens. It became a community gathering place where ecological innovation intermingled with lush vegetation. A mosaic Snake Bench and works of art designated a meeting area. Circular raised beds of colorful native California plants surround the commons of the Peralta Garden. It is widely used for meetings, workshops, and special events by neighbors and community organizations.

In 1999, Karl collaborated with community and environmental activists, city officials, and other supporters to establish Berkeley's EcoHouse, purchasing a small run-down residence, adjacent to the Karl Linn Community Garden, and transforming it into a model of affordable ecological technologies. EcoHouse is now a project of the Ecology Center.

Linn conceptualized the transformation of the nearby section of the Ohlone Greenway into an interpretive exhibit of the natural and cultural history of the area. Artists, teachers, designers, engineers, and native plant restorationists worked tirelessly to develop and construct exhibits that evoke the Spanish ranchero period, the agricultural era, and the rich culture of the Ohlone people, who inhabited the area for at least 10,000 years. A twenty-four-yard-long mural "From Elk Tracks to BART Tracks" depicts the history of the neighborhood from pre-settlement to the present, serving as an enormous picture book and inspiring passers-by to stop, reflect, and converse.

This cluster of commons projects contributes to the social and ecological vitality of the Westbrae neighborhood and is maintained and developed by the volunteer Friends of the Westbrae Commons. In 2003, filmmaker Rick Bacigalupi released his hour-long documentary *A Lot in Common* chronicling the planning and construction of the Peralta Community Art Garden and Commons. The film has aired on public television stations nationally and film festivals internationally.

The Bancroft Library at UC Berkeley recorded Linn's oral history, and his archives are housed at the UC Berkeley College of Environmental Design. He had a day dedicated to him by the City of Berkeley. Many of his projects are documented in his book *Building Commons and Community* (New Village Press, 2007).

# Appendix 6

# LYRICS

# ALBION
### (Nicole Milner)

It's a fishing village by the sea
It's a place I always like to be
Rolling meadows where the sheep do roam
Albion is my true home
Salmon creeks are down below
Where the fern and alder grow
Blue jays sing to me at dawn
Sunsets make me feel reborn
    Albion, oh Albion
      Thank you Lord for Albion

Pouring rains they wash so clean
On the days that feel so serene
And the fog makes colors bright
Then the sun it shines so light
Redwood trees they rise so high
You can hear the seagulls cry
Ocean sounds are always there
In the night the stars are clear
    Albion, oh Albion
      Thank you Lord for Albion

Albion means the white light
Just to know it feels so right
And everywhere we go
As its river we will flow
It's a fishing village by the sea
It's a place I always like to be
Rolling meadows where the sheep do roam
Albion is my true home
    Albion, oh Albion
      Thank you Lord for Albion

# BE THAT ONE

*(Nomi Yah, Ameir Smith, Mike Lounibos)*

I've been my brother's keeper most of our lives
He's been in and out of trouble many times
When he says he's changed, everybody rolls their eyes
They all tell me to give up, there's no getting through
The only thing that I know I can do is
    Be that one who prays
    Be that one who prays for the changes
    The Lord has the power to make
    Be that one who prays

In my brother there's a good man who wants out
He's still fighting when he's going down
I've seen him hold it together, then throw it all away
It's enough to make you wonder
Where's God in all of this
I've got to hand things over and bow my head
    Be that one who prays
    Be that one who prays for the changes
    The Lord has the power to make
    Be that one who prays

For the changes the Lord has the power to make
All the strength that we get with the gift of faith
When we ask him, answers come our way
When we choose to
    Be that one who prays
    Be that one who prays for the changes
    The Lord has the power to make
    Be that one who prays, be that one

# BENEFITS
*(Nomi Yah)*

I ask for a kiss and nothing more
Get your cheek going out the door
That's just a gesture
You act like you don't even believe in love
Like it's a thing you're suspicious of
While you make a plan to be my man
Without promising anything, without promising anything
      Is there a way that I could alter your point of view
      Prove to you the benefits
      Is there a way that I could offer you comfort to
      Demonstrate the benefits
      Don't underestimate the benefits of being in love
      Benefits of being in love

You ask why I'm tripping about this thing
Is it because of a wedding ring
That's just a symbol
You act so superior, unimpressed
Love's inferior at its best
A myth to cling to
Confident that you're
Not missing anything, not missing anything
      Is there a way that I could alter your point of view
      Prove to you the benefits
      Is there a way that I could offer you comfort to
      Demonstrate the benefits
      Don't underestimate the benefits of being in love
      Benefits of being in love

# BOOK OF LIFE
*(Nomi Yah)*

I dreamed of a vocal booth
Finishing an album with the youth
Taking my headphones off I left the room
Talking outside in the hallway to a luminous
Being shining like the moon
Couldn't see him, that's how much he shone
When I woke, I was filled with hope and with joy
Not with yesterday's sorrow

> Face of light, I never knew someone could
> Be so bright, I believe it was an angel that I
> Saw last night as it was written in the
> Book of Life where everything's written and
> Nothing's wiped, from the beginning to the
> End of time in the Book of Life

When Twitcher passed away from suicide
A week or two before I heard he died
I dreamed of the Book of Life
Written about Twitcher's life
I dreamed a sentence filled with light
And before I woke I read the type and it said
"And the light went out, like a handshake extended to no one."

> Face of light, I never knew someone could
> Be so bright, I believe it was an angel that I
> Saw last night as it was written in the
> Book of Life where everything's written and
> Nothing's wiped, from the beginning to the
> End of time in the Book of Life

Kindness of strangers seems to be
Anonymous angels protecting me
Keeping me from dangers, sheltering me
Cradling in mangers, swaddling me
I don't believe angels have big white wings
I don't believe angels lounge in heaven
And I don't believe angels look
Like church artists paint them
Like pictures portray them
> Face of light, I never knew someone could
> Be so bright, I believe it was an angel that I
> Saw last night as it was written in the
> Book of Life where everything's written and
> Nothing's wiped, from the beginning to the
> End of time in the Book of Life

# EXISTING
*(Nomi Yah, Adam Traum, Mike Lounibos)*

I hear everyone telling me to follow my heart
What if I don't even know what I want
The way it seems, dreams are moving targets
Why do I get obsessed about screwing things up
Frying my brain cells, thinking too much
I should just shut up and get something started
> We've gotta act to have an impact
> Can't go through the motions existing
> Get the job done, period
> Break the gridlock and give our hopes a shot at
> Existing, existing, existing

Only people who can't, say it can't be done
People who are hurt, try to hurt someone
Don't want to get sucked in to that way of thinking
So no matter what happens, I'm not gonna stop
Ramping my game up a hell of a lot
If I do nothing, I'll achieve nothing
> We've gotta act to have an impact
> Can't go through the motions existing
> Get the job done, period
> Break the gridlock and give our hopes a shot at
> Existing, existing, existing

How can time be wasted doing whatever
As long as we're trying to make the world better
I like to think being here matters
Helping someone up a rung on a ladder
> We've gotta act to have an impact
> Can't go through the motions existing
> Get the job done, period
> Break the gridlock and give our hopes a shot at
> Existing, existing, existing

# I Want You
## *(Nomi Yah)*

The thing is, once I had everything
A person needs, but I wasn't satisfied
Until I lost almost everything
Not for want of trying, Lord knows I tried
I wandered days, weeks, months and years
Top to bottom, mountains to oceans
Searching for ways make it through another day
Looking for ways to soothe emotions
  And now something is different
  Something is possible with you
  If you feel something for me too
  If you feel certain like I do
  I can't be certain about you
  But I know something about me
  I'm for certain, I want you

A long time passed, I wasn't afraid
To be alone, I hoped it was just for now
It's not like I didn't have offers, I had plenty
Men nice, decent good-looking abound
Heard various proposals, but I didn't wanna
Take the first train leaving out
I told myself, later on I'll be happy, I told myself
Later on I'll be in love, and I was right
  'Cause now something is different
  Something is possible with you
  If you feel something for me too
  If you feel certain like I do
  I can't be certain about you
  But I know something about me
  I'm for certain, I want you

And when you put your arms around me
I feel like snow feels on open flames
Butter feels in frying pans
Ice cream in falling rains
And when you put your arms around me
It's like there's really happy endings
At least you make my days happier
Waking in your arms in the mornings
      And now something is different
      Something is possible with you
      If you feel something for me too
      If you feel certain like I do
      I can't be certain about you
      But I know something about me
      I'm for certain, I want you

# I'M INSPIRED
### *(Nomi Yah)*

He's in the zone before the starting gun
Explodes and shows the world that he can run
See how he rockets through an opening in the crowd
They pile up but he's already out
Push to the limit, that's how to bring it
Until horns sound off across the finish line
>I'm inspired, setting a high bar
>It takes everything to win the race
>There's no second place
>I'm inspired, motivated to try hard
>I'm on fire, I'm inspired

She helps the poor disadvantaged youth
She volunteers for forty years to do it
She could have given up and gotten out anytime
She lives so they can have a better life
Push to the limit, that's how to bring it
Until horns sound off across the finish line
>I'm inspired, setting a high bar
>It takes everything to win the race
>There's no second place
>I'm inspired, motivated to try hard
>I'm on fire, I'm inspired

To my heroes, my examples
I say thank you, thank you
Thank you, thank you
>I'm inspired, setting a high bar
>It takes everything to win the race
>There's no second place
>I'm inspired, motivated to try hard
>I'm on fire, I'm inspired

# IF YOU'RE ALIVE
*(Nomi Yah)*

If you're alive, send a message, dial a telephone
Five-five-five seven-one-oh-six, same number as before
The last I heard, they found your car in North Mexico
If you're alive, let me know
      Did you make it through the hard times
      Did it all turn out OK
      I never did forget you
      And I wonder to this day
      If you're alive, if you're alive

You got paranoid, saying that we had to leave at dawn
Or we'd be destroyed, were you high or crazy or both
What the hell went wrong
The last time you were ever seen
You were begging me to go
Shedding a tear when I said no
      Did you make it through the hard times
      Did it all turn out OK
      I never did forget you
      And I wonder to this day
      If you're alive, if you're alive

You're a dot dot dot
An unfinished thought
I don't want to let this go
I just have to know
      If you're alive, if you're alive

# INSIDE MY HEAD
### (Nomi Yah)

The tune you heard in my studio
Was like no other you heard before
My sound's unique and extraordinary
      I have to find my own way
         'Though I have to pay my own way
         I'll make it one way or ninety-nine other ways
         Something's going on inside my head

I left your name at the front door
You caught my act at the stage show
You didn't know I'm extraordinary
      I have to find my own way
         'Though I have to pay my own way
         I'll make it one way or ninety-nine other ways
         Something's going on inside my head

If you lift me up I'll kiss the skies
If we win the game we split the prize
If you want to play, then I'll say your name
At the Grammy's
      I have to find my own way
         'Though I have to pay my own way
         I'll make it one way or ninety-nine other ways
         Something's going on inside my head

# LIFE ALONE
*(Nomi Yah, Andrew Milne, Mike Lounibos)*

You're sitting by yourself again
And if you had some better friends
You wouldn't push them all away
But who the hell am I to say
It's like you never understand
It's like I'm just a grain of sand
Or at least, that's the impression I get
When your pupils reflect
That no one treats you right
    You don't have to live your life alone, hey no
    You don't have to live your life alone

Welcome to the human race
Where isolation is a waste
I'm looking for a sign of life
And getting nothing in your eyes
I never know what I should say
And you're a universe away
Or at least, that's the impression I get
When your pupils reflect
You're all torn up inside
    You don't have to live your life alone, hey no
    You don't have to live your life alone
    You don't have to live your life alone, hey no
    You don't have to live your life alone
    And neither do I

'Cause even though you feel like you're on your own
You don't have to live your life alone

# MORE PRECIOUS
*(Nomi Yah)*

I won't leave you, I could never leave you
You are always with me, I love your face
If I left you, I would be without you
I would lose a treasure nothing could replace
      You are more precious than gold
      You are more precious than silver
      I will cherish you always

I will give you all my colors
All my darkness, all my light
If you'll take me, I will never leave you
You are always with me, day and night
      You are more precious than gold
      You are more precious than silver
      I will cherish you always
      You are more precious to me

I won't leave you, I could never leave you
I would lose a treasure nothing could replace
      You are more precious than gold
      You are more precious than silver
      I will cherish you always
      You are more precious to me

# Napalm Gardens
*(Nomi Yah)*

Did you ever hear about Napalm Gardens
A little place behind the family house
The sun never shines in Napalm Gardens
You never really know who's alive in the corners

You're the one who comes to Napalm Gardens
Maybe it's Tuesday night, you hear there's a party
At a place called Napalm Gardens
There is no light, you're not sure this is the right place

You're opening the door to Napalm Gardens
A man asks you for a dollar, but he says,
"You don't have to pay in Napalm Gardens
Just pay attention" and he pulls you inside

There's one electric light bulb in a room painted black
A couple dozen people acting like they're on drugs
One's kissing the head of a doll
One's carving a cross on the wall
It's some underground scene
Like you've never seen on TV
One boy, cross-eyed and pale
Tells you he just got out of jail
Gives you a piece of bubble gum and says
"Man, where did you come from?"
And you're still wondering
Is this the right party?

Singer takes the mic, puts it in his mouth
The boy's f***zed up, put so many holes in himself
He's leaking on the girl with spikes on her wrists
Dancing her fists hard into your face

Young junked prophet lying on the concrete
Spitting prophecies all over your shoes says,
"You don't understand me, nothing I say is true
There is no truth"

Your best friend just came into Napalm Gardens
Singer looks up, there's white in his eyes
He drops the microphone onto the floor
Runs out the back door and hides until morning

And he'll say, "I thought they were the cops"
F***ed up boy, put so many holes in himself
And he's leaking leaking leaking leaking
Leaking leaking leaking leaking
Leaking leaking leaking all over
Napalm Gardens, Napalm Gardens
Napalm Gardens, Napalm Gardens
Napalm

# PARIS TO ME
## *(Nomi Yah)*

I see Paris at night, the air is painted colors
In the neon light, the city is a dream
Café's are laughing as I pass
Inviting me to take a glass
And join their potpourri, Paris to me

J'ne parle pas and ou et la Metro
Walk the street 'til dawn, the city never sleeps
The Eiffel tower cuts the sky
The Mona Lisa passes by
This is the place to be, Paris to me

Hold your baguette over your shoulder
Try some Camembert
If you sing, you'll never get older
Why not leave your cares
Come on in, forget your sorrow
There may never be tomorrow
Cross the Seine, Notre Dame bells pealing
Drink champagne, the party's reeling
Throw the dice, this is your night
Music's nice, the setting's right
Tears are not the Paris style
If you can fake your French
You can fake a smile

I see Paris by day, the rain is pouring down
In a cheap café I'm sitting far from home
I'm a stranger, I'm alone
I wish that I could go back home
I wish there was a sea between Paris and me

# Perfect Enough
*(Nomi Yah)*

Your child gets tall, while you are busy
Think of it, isn't it really a shame
If you miss it all, childhood is brief
Picture books and loose teeth
And that Little League game, man, relax
    Life is perfect enough, perfect enough
    Lord, it could be better
    Sometimes it's rough
    But today is perfect enough

Your Jaguar's fast but you're running late
You won't catch the plane, you'll just get on the next
And you'll fly first-class, trying to achieve
The American Dream
While you're piling up debts, man, relax
    Life is perfect enough, perfect enough
    Lord, it could be better
    Sometimes it's rough
    But today is perfect enough

You should be proud of what you've done
Look how far you've come

It's all a matter of priority, keep up what you're doing
If it doesn't ruin the time that you spend
With your family, you are their rock
And they love when you walk
Through that door at the end of the day
    Life is perfect enough, perfect enough
    Lord, it could be better
    Sometimes it's rough
    But today is perfect enough

# Rows Of Roses
*(Nomi Yah)*

When Grandpa proposed, he gave her a rose
On their wedding day, he gave a big bouquet
On anniversaries, he went to nurseries
Every year he chose a different color rose
To put in the ground for her
For fifty years
>She has rows of roses, growing in her garden
>She has rows of roses, planted in her yard
>She cuts and puts them in a vase
>It puts a smile on her face
>To see those rows and rows of roses

As Grandpa would say, a store-bought bouquet
Doesn't last for long, now even though he's gone
He still gives flowers to her
For the rest of her years
>She has rows of roses, growing in her garden
>She has rows of roses, planted in her yard
>She cuts and puts them in a vase
>It puts a smile on her face
>To see those rows and rows of roses

We said come live with us, she wouldn't budge
She decided to stay where she was
Where she could breathe his undying love
His undying love
>She cuts and puts them in a vase
>It puts a smile on her face
>To see those rows and rows of roses

# SECOND CHANCE
### *(Nomi Yah)*

Don't think for a second, it's a given, no it's not
It's a privilege, not a right, to be forgiven, you'd better not
Have password-protected phone numbers
Different screen names you go under
Double lives, second wives, don't want a song and dance
    If you want a second chance with me
    Prove your love to me, buy me jewelry
    Like you promised me, flowers and groceries
    Fall down on your knees, beg me, baby please
    If you want a second chance

Don't make me turn into a third wheel, that's not me
Don't think of yourself, think how I feel, I won't be
A spare pair of sunglasses
Unplugged appliances
Won't be number two under no circumstance
    If you want a second chance with me
    Prove your love to me, buy me jewelry
    Like you promised me, flowers and groceries
    Fall down on your knees, beg me, baby please
    If you want a second chance

You won't get a third, three-strikes and you're out
I hope that you heard and figured it out
First time you screw up, your number's up
You better be good, you better be good
You better be good
    If you want a second chance with me
    Prove your love to me, buy me jewelry
    Like you promised me, flowers and groceries
    Fall down on your knees, beg me, baby please
    If you want a second chance

# SEEMS LIKE A MOVIE
### *(Nomi Yah)*

If I tell you rain is falling and my tears are falling too
You'd be like, yeah right, but God believe me, it's true
If I tell you thunder's shaking and my body's shaking too
You'd be like, yeah right, but God believe me, it's true
  Romeo & Juliet must be in love
  But it's over between them
  Where does that leave them
  Poisoned and laying out there
  If this was Shakespeare or a movie theater
  I'd buy tickets
  If I tell you how I feel
  Seems like a movie but its real

If I tell you lightning's cracking and my heart is cracking too
You'd be like, yeah right, but God believe me, it's true
If I even came close to saying how much I'm missing you
You'd be like, yeah right, but God believe me, it's true
  Romeo & Juliet must be in love
  But it's over between them
  Where does that leave them
  Poisoned and laying out there
  If this was Shakespeare or a movie theater
  I'd buy tickets
  If I tell you how I feel
  Seems like a movie but its real

# SHE HUGGED HIM
*(Nomi Yah)*

Christopher enlisted to get out of the house
Paychecks and tuition outweighed all the doubts
His dad had never been this proud
But his mom broke down
      She hugged him a long time
      She hugged him and didn't let go
      His memory took a photo
      She hugged him and didn't let go

Christopher got orders when he was newlywed
His wife was smiling, while her eyes were red
She wore a yellow silk shirt
Whispered, please don't get hurt
      She hugged him a long time
      She hugged him and didn't let go
      His memory took a photo
      She hugged him and didn't let go

All those pictures in his mind
Got him through all those months of extended time

Christopher was wounded, but it got even worse
When he got papers asking for divorce
He took his Purple Heart home
And gave it to his mom
      She hugged him a long time
      She hugged him and didn't let go
      She hugged him

# SHRIMP-FRIED RICE
## *(Nomi Yah)*

You're the only one who really
Really really checks for me
Most people don't even get close enough
To even get next to me
You write me a rhyme, you find me the time
You're never too vexed with me
You write me a poem, you follow me home
You know how to flex with me
When I'm hungry, you spend your money
Buying shrimp-fried rice for me
When I'm sick with a fever, you get lemon-squeezer
Mix sugar, water & ice for me
When I'm lonely, you call on the phone
And the tone of your voice is nice to me
When I'm getting unsure, you're giving encouragement
Good advice to me
      If I was in Paradise, I would be home
      I would be holding you, I would be holding you

You're surprising me when you detail
Vacuum, wash and gas my car
You're surprising with a Sobe
And an orange chocolate bar
You're satisfied, don't want me to change
You like the way things are
In your eyes, I'm a super-hero
Diva and a superstar
You super-size and tantalize me
With a shopping spree
You personalize and customize
My name with embroidery
When people outside us try to divide us

'Cause of jealousy
When they try to bribe us, you take my side
They can't take you away from me
> If I was in Paradise, I would be home
> I would be holding you, I would be holding you

You're an individual who can't be defined
Can't be denied
You're ever so loyal, never ignore me
Keeping me by your side
'Though people may think whatever they think
I know I'm your bona fide
Whenever we part, I know in my heart
We'll again and again collide
You're an independent who can't be controlled
You're wild inside
If people just knew you like I know you
They would be surprised
Who cares about them, you and I are best friends
In one another we confide
I prayed, God responded, how we're bonded
Has me mystified
> If I was in Paradise, I would be home
> I would be holding you, I would be holding you

You're the only one who really really
Really checks for me
Most people don't even get close enough
To even get next to me
You write me a rhyme, you find me the time
You're never too vexed with me
You write me a poem, you follow me home
You know how to flex with me
When I'm hungry, you spend your money
Buying shrimp-fried rice

# Slow Down
*(Nomi Yah)*

So many songs in an afternoon
Your head's running round with an evening tune
Inspiration is gathering momentum
You're breaking the speed limit, hitting your stride
Lyrics are leaking out of your pen
You look at the clock, it's a quarter to ten
Heavenly angels give you their compositions
You're going too fast, can you finish the song
    Slow down, don't forget to breathe
    Don't forget to see the sky
    Don't forget to live
    Don't forget to laugh a little
    Don't forget to cry

Take a break and relax awhile
Have a cup of tea and we'll crack a smile
Go on a run when you wake up in the morning
Open a window, throw a water balloon
Is it your obligation
To get the most from your inspiration
Will songs be lost if you don't write them down
You'll lose sight of yourself if you keep going on
    Slow down, don't forget to breathe
    Don't forget to see the sky
    Don't forget to live
    Don't forget to laugh a little
    Don't forget to cry

# SUCH A GOOD THING
### *(Nomi Yah)*

Clocks are stuck and fluctuating
Melting like a Dali painting
I can't find a clock that won't stick
Each one mocks me, tick-tick-tick-tick
Ticking slowly, every second
Only felons have time to reckon
I spend all my time trying to survive
You remind me why I'm alive
      Your love is such a good thing
      Love will be the last thing we immortalize
      When lives flash before our eyes
      Love is such a good thing
      Such a good thing, such a good thing

Grains of sand in hourglasses
When you're gone, time never passes
Passing time is all I do
Until I get to be with you
I'm waiting for the minute you come home
As if you were the rising sun
Tension in my body and my mind
A touch of your hand and I unwind
      Your love is such a good thing
      Love will be the last thing we immortalize
      When lives flash before our eyes
      Love is such a good thing
      Such a good thing, such a good thing
      Such a good thing, such a good thing
      Such a good thing, such a good thing
      Such a good thing

# THE WAY HE LEFT

*(Nomi Yah, John Mazzei)*

Too many signs I wasn't seeing
He started fights without a reason
Kept getting louder, making zero sense
Face turning redder, looking too intense
He canceled meals, while I was waiting
Not answering when I was calling
I kept on feeling like a roller coaster
I was being ghosted

> The way he left wasn't right
> Took off without any warning
> Like a thief in the night
> The way he left wasn't right
> He said he didn't want to talk
> Because he didn't want to fight
> He could've been braver sooner than later
> Conversation could've done us both a favor
> The way he left wasn't right, the way he left

When I got home, felt something wrong
I looked around, his stuff was gone
Half-empty closet like a missing tooth
He didn't leave a note and no excuse
Some months had passed, he called and he said
He wants me back, he made a mistake
Rule number one in a relationship is don't abandon ship

> The way he left wasn't right
> Took off without any warning
> Like a thief in the night
> The way he left wasn't right
> He said he didn't want to talk
> Because he didn't want to fight
> He could've been braver sooner than later
> Conversation could've done us both a favor
> The way he left wasn't right, the way he left

# THIRD WORLD AMERICAN
*(Nomi Yah)*

Third World American and poor of all nations
Living in poverty and discrimination
Third-world American in this situation
To survive when deprived is suffering, yeah
But even oppressors are feeling oppression
Voluntary slavery to increase their possessions
Third-world American is dissatisfied
In this state of emergency, angels have cried
    Oh, we will get there, people, and we shall over
    We shall overcome

Third-world American, what have we got
You see that some have nothing and some have a lot
Some live in a yacht, some in a parking lot
Some are biting the bullet, some are calling the shot
And there are those who have thought
That those who have not, should have fought but forgot
Or maybe they never got taught
But blaming the victim is a habit of thought
Like asking a fish in the market, how come you got caught
    Oh, come on, people, and we shall over
    We shall overcome

Poor people are angry with reason a' plenty
'Cause one person's riches leave another one empty
We've got to stop the military taking more
Taking from the basic needs of the American poor
We've got to stop the business of making war
Equality and justice, that's what we're asking for
Third-world American, rise above
We've got to build a global morality based in love
    Oh, we are waiting and we shall over
    We shall overcome

# WAIT

*(Nomi Yah, John Mazzei)*

Right up close, looking at each other
Like looking through a microscope
That's no joke, anything goes viral
And privacy is on the ropes
Social media's feeding you make-believe
Feeding you make-believe
Quit that flaming and blaming and talk to me
    Wait, wait, let me explain
    You've got misinformation
    Slamming through your brain
    Leaving a path of damage like a hurricane
    Wait, wait, let me explain
    Now can you please stop raging, going on and on
    Listen to me, it's obvious you've got it wrong

You look tense, it must've been a shocker
To see me with somebody else
That makes sense, I get how you're feeling
Your heart is pumping, beating fast
You keep yelling and telling me about a post
Telling me about a post
    You Wait, wait, let me explain
    You've got misinformation
    Slamming through your brain
    Leaving a path of damage like a hurricane
    Wait, wait, let me explain
    Now can you please stop raging, going on and on
    Listen to me, it's obvious you've got it wrong

See that photograph, there in the post
From so far back, it's like a ghost
Way in the past when I was younger
Show some class and don't act so dumb
    Wait, wait, let me explain
    You've got misinformation
    Slamming through your brain
    Leaving a path of damage like a hurricane
    Wait, wait, let me explain
    Now can you please stop raging, going on and on
    Listen to me, it's obvious you've got it wrong

A million words don't matter when they aren't true
There's only one word that I keep on telling you
Wait

# WEEKENDS
*(Nomi Yah, John Mazzei)*

I keep my head down, making an income
I've got a day job, most of us do
The hours pass by a little faster
When there's a paycheck waiting for you
Fridays are boring us, 'til quitting time
Mondays come back fast, in record time
    Let's get out of here and grab our freedom
    That's why they created weekends
    Let's get epic, go off the deep end
    That's why they created weekends

Wish I could sleep in, but there's a meeting
Seems like we always have to work
I'm not complaining, but I'm explaining
I've gotta get that life I deserve
Fridays are boring us, 'til quitting time
Mondays come back fast, in record time
    Let's get out of here and grab our freedom
    That's why they created weekends
    Let's get epic, go off the deep end
    That's why they created weekends

When we go out driving we don't even read the signs
We end up where we are when we get out of the car
I feel like, this is the kind of day that all our
Daydreams are made of
If we make the most of it and get a little
Uninhibited, a little lit now
    Let's get out of here and grab our freedom
    That's why they created weekends
    Let's get epic, go off the deep end
    That's why they created weekends

# WHAT ARE WE GIVING SANTA
### (Nomi Yah, Mike Lounibos)

He has every toy that was ever made
And he only wears the one red suit
Maybe if we knew what his shoe size was
We could buy him a new pair of boots
And he doesn't need a new razor blade
'Cause he never ever has a shave
Wish we had enough for a pickup truck
So he wouldn't have to drive a sleigh, hey hey hey
>Christmas morning's almost here
>What are we giving Santa, what are we giving Santa
>He brings presents every year
>What are we giving Santa

We got bales of hay for the reindeer team
We sent Mrs. Clause a big bouquet
Every Santa's elf gets a new green hat
Sugar cookies on a golden plate
It'd be fun to throw him a party
But he'll only come when we're asleep
If we were as smart as the three wise men
We could figure out what to bring, hey hey hey
>Christmas morning's almost here
>What are we giving Santa, what are we giving Santa
>He brings presents every year
>What are we giving Santa

Look there a gift for you, here's one for me
How come there's nothing for Santa under the tree
>Christmas morning's almost here
>What are we giving Santa, what are we giving Santa
>He brings presents every year
>What are we giving Santa

# WHEN IT'S MAGIC
*(Nomi Yah, Ron Brown)*

I shredded when I should have filed
And broke the fax machine
The boss went off but I didn't mind
'Cause it was six-fifteen
I said, Sorry, I wasn't paying attention
My mind is stuck on someone
It's crazy what happens
> When it's magic, love appears in thin air
> Loneliness disappears
> I'm distracted, that's a classic reaction
> When it's magic

I was flying down the road
Didn't see the stop sign
When a cop brought me back to earth
A four hundred dollar fine
I said, Sorry, I wasn't paying attention
My mind is stuck on someone
It's crazy what happens
> When it's magic, love appears in thin air
> Loneliness disappears
> I'm distracted, that's a classic reaction
> When it's magic

The experience is so intense
It goes against common sense
> When it's magic, love appears in thin air
> Loneliness disappears
> I'm distracted, that's a classic reaction
> When it's magic

# WHEN SOMEONE DOESN'T LOVE YOU
### (Nomi Yah)

There's a chandelier on the ceiling
While the sun is in the sky
Oriental rugs on hardwood floors
While wildflowers grow outside
We built a castle, a fairytale
We did our best, but it had to fail
It was never real
> When someone doesn't love you, you can tell
> You see it in their eyes, you know them so well
> It's hard to make changes that hurt like hell
> Don't want to let go, but you might as well
> When someone doesn't love you

We should talk about our feelings
When we don't we're telling lies
Haven't had a fight or anything
This must come as a surprise
Doesn't matter how much I care
We can't make love when no love is there
How can we breathe with no air
> When someone doesn't love you, you can tell
> You see it in their eyes, you know them so well
> It's hard to make changes that hurt like hell
> Don't want to let go, but you might as well

Birds can't even fly unless they spread their wings and try
And take a risk to reach the sky
Then they can finally be free
Life is passing by, we have to live before we die
Know when it's time to say goodbye
Knowing that this was meant to be, this was meant to be
      When someone doesn't love you, you can tell
      You see it in their eyes, you know them so well
      It's hard to make changes that hurt like hell
      You don't want to let go, but you might as well
      When someone doesn't love you

# White Collar Criminal
### *(Nomi Yah)*

A teenager has a toy gun, robs a liquor store
Takes twenty twenty-dollar bills
Twenty minutes later, face down on the pavement
Twenty months later he's still
Still in lockdown and across town, pocketing twenty mil
A CEO makes out like a thief
Knowing someone else'll foot the bill
Someone else'll foot the bill
    White-collar criminal gets away with it
    He gets a slap on, slap on, slap on the wrist
    And the one who's innocent is the one who pays
    He gets a slap in, slap in, slap in the face
    White-collar criminal, white-collar criminal

A man never gets a leg up, never takes a hand out
Never has a lucky break
Saves every penny, pays down debts
Puts the rest in an IRA
Hoping to retire at sixty-five
It's getting him through the days
He's almost there when it all disappears
And it's gone without a trace, gone without a trace
    White-collar criminal gets away with it
    He gets a slap on, slap on, slap on the wrist
    And the one who's innocent is the one who pays
    He gets a slap in, slap in, slap in the face

Now I'm a patriot, but I'm not an idiot
And when our system fails, the wrong one's sent to jail
That makes me mad as hell, it makes me mad as hell
White-collar criminal, white-collar criminal

White-collar criminal gets away with it
He gets a slap on, slap on, slap on the wrist
And the one who's innocent is the one who pays
He gets a slap in, slap in, slap in the face
White-collar criminal, white-collar criminal

# Woman To Woman
*(Nomi Yah, Eva Snyder)*

I saw your name when his cell lit up
I had to call, I'm glad you picked up
Let's get the story straight
Fill in the blanks, rip off the bandaid
Every night he spends with me
Is he telling you he's busy
Does he pretend I'm just a friend, that's bull
      I'm not trying to make you feel bad
      I'm not the one to get mad at
      My words might hit you like a bullet
      Hey, don't shoot the messenger
      It's just a lesson learned
      Dealing with this, woman to woman

Couldn't say I saw it coming
Me and him spent hours talking
Drinking and smoking, I believed in
Everything he was saying
He had one foot out the exit
I'm a fool who never knew it
I took the bait, I drank the Kool-Aid
      I'm not trying to make you feel bad
      I'm not the one to get mad at
      My words might hit you like a bullet
      Hey, don't shoot the messenger
      It's just a lesson learned
      Dealing with this s**t, woman to woman

We have to stop this, he took it way too far
Now here we are
> I'm not trying to make you feel bad
> I'm not the one to get mad at
> My words might hit you like a bullet
> Hey, don't shoot the messenger
> It's just a lesson learned
> Dealing with this, woman to woman

www.ingramcontent.com/pod-product-compliance
Lightning Source LLC
Chambersburg PA
CBHW021810170526
45157CB00007B/2534